Better than Sex
ARJUNA ARDAGH

The Ecstatic art of Awakening Coaching.

Published by Awakening Coaching LLC
420 Nursery St Nevada City CA 95959
http://awakeningcoachingtraining.com

ISBN: 978-1-890909-48-2

For my colleagues and students
in Awakening Coaching
all over the world.
May you touch many hearts

TABLE OF CONTENTS

THE READERS WEBSITE

You might not have known it at the time, but when you bought this book, as an ebook or as a physical book, you also bought yourself a membership to a readers website.

It does not cost you any extra, you just need to go and register. Once you have created your membership, you will get additional access to video, audio, additional reading materials and other goodies.

You will need the order number from your purchase on iTunes, Amazon or from our website.

You can register here: http://arjunaardagh.com/bts-register

And there is even more good news. If you would later like to get coached by one of our coaches, take a group coaching course, or to train to become a coach, you can get a discount of the same amount as you paid for this book. So if you choose to do more, this book was free!

This slender book will change your life. It will expand your capacity for joy and happiness, give you tools for navigating life's challenges, and offer a method for profoundly affecting the lives of others…all while getting paid for it as a coach.

I experienced Arjuna's revolutionary way of delivering these benefits a few years ago when he invited me to attend his Awakening Coaching Training. Since you are about to embark on a similar journey through this book, I'd like to share the remarkable things I found there.

After 34 years of executive coaching and 48 years of daily mind-body practices, I no longer judge teachers by the quality of their presentations. There are many powerful teachers of wisdom whose presence on the stage is inspiring. And while Arjuna does well by that standard, it's how quickly his students learn and how immediately they begin to guide others that set his teaching apart.

In Arjuna's training, my classmates were like the math student who came late to class, copied a problem from the board, and solved it as homework. Apparently he hadn't heard the professor say it was unsolvable. Arjuna's students were similarly unencumbered by imagined limitations, and it's part of the reason they learned so easily.

Too often the great teachings are presented as mysterious and inscrutable. While it's true that the depth of what we discover through learning the Open Secret takes time to mature and integrate into our lives, access to the source of that wisdom can be immediate because it's already within us.

One reason Arjuna's students find that source so quickly is that his classes are fun. Considering the piousness with which much spiritual teaching is marbled, a little fun is indeed a relief. But it also creates an environment for accelerated learning. Learning our mother tongue in our first two years of life is a magnificent feat, which largely happens through play and experimentation. Arjuna takes care to amplify those elements of delight and discovery for his students.

I have no doubt that you can progress rapidly, as well. This material is tried and true. Whether Open Secret wisdom with its attendant happiness is actually better than sex is for you to decide. That inquiry may require extensive research on your part, but I assume you possess the dedication to see it through.

In the mean time, you have in your hands an invitation to an experience that is both playful and profound. While Arjuna's style of writing is casual, it is also precise and clear. This book opens the door to a journey of discovery filled with wonder and wisdom. May its benefits extend to all those whose lives you touch.

Stephen Josephs
co-author of Leadership Agility and author of Dragons at Work
Novato, CA
October, 2013

SECTION 1:

Welcome

CHAPTER 1

Drinks Are on The Deck

Welcome to my new book. Come on in. Let me take your things. There is a lot of fun stuff going on here, so we can have an excellent time together. There is dancing in the living room, a movie is showing in the basement, and drinks are on the deck. You can nibble on some radical new ideas in the kitchen, and you can test out some powerful tools in the garage, by yourself or with others. Hopefully, we will have a few good laughs along the way. If you like a good treasure hunt, we've got that, too. I have left little Web thingies (please excuse my techie geek-talk here) throughout the book with links to video, audio, and other goodies on a readers' website[1], exclusively for you and other guests at the party.

I'm glad that you came just as you are. No need to dress up. This is a very informal book. You might have already come to some of the other books I invited you to. Many of them had interviews with dozens of erudite people, and a bibliography that stretched all the way from the coat closet to the bathroom down the hall. Those were black tie events, with a catering service, valet parking, and a string quartet in the drawing room. But not so with this little Saturday afternoon barbecue book you have wandered into here. This is Arjuna Ardagh *chez moi* — in my flip flops, and shorts, and wrinkled Hawaiian shirt — just friends hanging out together. So come on in, make yourself at home: you'll fit right in. You can meet all the other people who showed up for the party here.[2]

---

[1] http://better-than-sex.kajabi.com/login
[2] http://better-than-sex.kajabi.com/groups/9763

I invited you here because I want to share something marvelous with you. I want to tell you about the Open Secret that I am most inspired by, grateful for, and passionate about. It is this that I like talking about the most, and relaxing into. I have dedicated my whole adult life to the praises of this Open Secret. I want to share with you here how easy it is for you to get yourself some of this same magical potion today—in fact how easy it is for anyone on the whole entire planet to enjoy it, here, now, just as we already are. And if that was not enough, I want to tell you how you can, very easily, become a vehicle for the Open Secret, a distributor, a disseminator, a flag-bearer, an active agent of splendor on the earth.

Now tell me, honestly, how cool is that?

Which brings me to the title. I am sure when you got the invitation to this book it must have aroused your curiosity. Some people have even showed up here who did not notice the "than" in the title.

"You Arjuna?" they ask me. I admit that I am. "Good, we got the invitation, and we are here to find out about…"—they look around furtively, and mumble out of the side of their pursed lips—"… better sex."

"Excuse me?" I ask them. "You want to find out about what?"

"Sex. We came here to find out about better sex." Finally, a deep breath of courage. "We want BETTER SEX," they blurt out, "and we want it now."

"Ah, I see. Well, no need to shout. It's an innocent mistake. No, actually the invitation said 'Better THAN Sex.' I can tell you all about the one thing that is better than sex. The Open Secret that is available to anyone, anywhere on the planet, right here, right now, that solves all your troubles instantly, and that gives you access to infinite creativity."

Despite the misunderstanding, some people take me up on the offer. Others remain quite adamant that what they really want is indeed Better Sex, and nothing more or less than that will do. I send them over to the party at John Gray's house. He has all the best supplements for Mars and Venus to get His and Her hormones dancing a wild tango on the grand piano. Lucky for all, it totally works (marsvenus.com), and so everyone is happy.

Now, you might assume that someone who has the brazen boldness, or the flagrant foolishness, to call his book Better Than Sex is probably just repressed and stuck up, and does not like sex very much. Since I am British by birth, it would indeed be a reasonable assumption. But that ain't me, babe. No, no, no. I love sex. Sex, sex, sexy wet wild delicious SEX. Yes please, over here, more for me, please. I have felt very positive about sex, despite my repressive British genes, for more than 42 years, and I plan to stay very enthusiastic indeed about sex for many more years to come. The secret that I want to tell you about here is so delicious, so powerful, so sweet, so incredibly fulfilling, so complete, so effective at soothing all your pain, breathing love and humor into your relationships, and lighting up your innate genius, that it is really hard to find words to express just how totally excellent it is. So just think of whatever you thought was the very peak of awesomeness so far (in my case, that would be sex), multiply it by 1,000, and there you have it: the Open Secret that we are talking about here.

Let me tell you a little more about this very good news, and how absurd it is that something more available to us than water, or air, or dirt, or cute kittens on Facebook, is not more popular than it actually is. *So far.*

For starters, The Open Secret never, ever, ever, gets boring. I first discovered it about 21 years ago, and I have had a good fix many times a day ever since. Every time it is totally new, never repetitive, like it is your very first time, every time. See what I mean? It is Better than Sex.

The Open Secret never needs upgrading, replacing, or fixing. Once you know where to find it, it stays as shiny and new as the day you first got it out of the box. It has no bugs, no incompatibilities with other programs; no virus can corrupt it.

Which, in fact, makes it not only better than sex, but better than the Macintosh Operating System as well, which is another of my favorite things.

If you are single, the Open Secret also comes in very handy indeed. Have you ever been to a party feeling really, *really* single? Like you need somebody, want somebody, yearn for somebody to make you whole again? As you may have noticed, that can be an unwise dating strategy. The more you long for Mr. or Ms. Right, the more needy you become, the more even semi-right people act indifferent. The Open Secret totally takes care of that. Just a few drops of the Open Secret under your tongue, and you become beautiful from the inside out. You become irresistibly magnetic, and gorgeous people show up in your life, out of thin air, wanting you. It worked for me: I am married to the queen of gorgeousness now, and I used to have trouble dating skunks. Which, incidentally, makes the Open Secret not only better than sex, but better than Coco Chanel No. 5 as well.

If you are in a relationship, the Open Secret also has magic to offer you. Do you ever get together with your partner for an intimate evening, and find yourselves fighting over random nonsense? Then the more you try to set it right, the deeper you dig the hole, or rather, the very separate two holes you now find yourselves in? The Open Secret will magically dissolve the feeling of separation between the two of you, so you just cannot, for the life of you both, remember what the fight was about. The Open Secret leaves you just separate enough to find each other interesting, exotic, and mysterious, and just merged enough to feel intimate, safe, and at home. Which makes the Open Secret better than Dr. Phil.

You may have heard that doctors tell us more than 85% of the ailments we suffer from are stress-related. Well, the Open Secret is the ultimate stress-buster.

If you are creative, the Open Secret unblocks the flow of the muse, so you become a relaxed scribe for a torrent of brilliance that just pours through you, and all you need to do is lounge by the pool sipping Mai Tais and download it all.

I could go on and on. In fact I think I will, for another couple of hundred pages or so, because the Open Secret has endless great things to be said about it.

I must admit that I am not the first person to write a book about the Open Secret, although I might be the first person to do so while lounging by a pool sipping Mai Tais. Just about every great, creative, and truly happy person throughout history has relied heavily upon the Open Secret for an endless supply of free energy.

By now you are probably wondering where you can get your own supply right away, and start to enjoy it for yourself. OK. So now I am going to tell you where to go, and where to look. The best way to do this is to remember one of those ancient texts about the Open Secret:

> Long ago, when the earth and all living creatures were being created, a meeting was called of the council of the Gods. They wanted to make the Open Secret available to all Human beings, but they were concerned that it might be misused. So they decided to hide it where only those people who could value its power could find it.
>
> Where to hide the Open Secret was the question. "Let's bury it deep in the earth," said one God. But another answered, "No, that will not do, because humans will eventually create huge machines to dig into the earth and find it."
>
> Another God said, "Let's sink it in the deepest ocean." But then came the objection, "No, not there, for they will learn to dive into the ocean in big metal fishes, and will find it." Then someone said, "Let's take it to the top of the highest mountain and hide it there." But once again another replied, "No, that will not do either, because they will eventually climb every mountain and put the Open Secret to improper use." Then they all gave up in despondency. "We do not know where to hide it, because it seems that there is no place on earth or in the sea that human beings will not eventually reach."

The King of all the Gods thought for a long time and then said, "Here is what we will do. We will hide the Open Secret deep in the center of their own being, for humans will never think to look for it there."

They all agreed that this was the perfect hiding place, and the deed was done. Since that time, humans have been going up and down the earth, digging, diving, climbing, and exploring, searching for power and riches and resources, when all the time the greatest treasure is already within themselves.

This book is all about how to uncover the Open Secret that is hidden deep within all of us. And, more important, it is about how to perform the ultimate act of service and loving kindness that anyone could possibly perform for any other human being: bringing the Open Secret alive in another....

In this book, I am going to tell you about how to do this in general terms. I am going to describe for you the seven qualities that anyone can develop to become an excellent support to anyone else in this way. But I am also going to make frequent reference to a particular method which we have developed, called Awakening Coaching, which makes these seven qualities activated and available in anyone who wants to use them. This is a little bit like Steve Jobs writing a book about what it takes to create a really great computer, or Henry Ford writing a book about the internal combustion engine. They could each write about basic principles, but of course they would end up referencing Apple computers or Ford motor cars a good deal as well, to add credibility and examples. I will tell you all that you need to know here about how to bring forth The Open Secret in anyone else, and I will also illustrate this with how we do it using the tools of Awakening Coaching.

Our exploration must start with you. Remember that this party is a potluck, right? I see that you are clutching something very delicious in that container you are holding. This is the most important ingredient of all. Follow me into the kitchen, and let us start right here, with what you brought to the party.

CHAPTER 2

What About You?

E verything begins and ends with you. To be useful and relevant and worthy of your time, it *has* to begin with you.

There is a reason why you showed up here at my place today. You could be doing so many other things right now. You could be watching *Modern Family* on your TV, reading *Fifty Shades of Gray*, gambling futures on the stock exchange, feeding the homeless, or visiting your parents. You could be walking in nature, or water skiing, or bungee jumping, or knitting a wooly hat for a kitten. You could be on Facebook, posting, and liking and sharing pictures of kittens in your small wooly hats. You could be drinking, smoking, eating, dancing, or pole vaulting. But you are doing none of those things, are you? Be honest with me. You are not skydiving right now, or scuba diving, or giving a speech at the United Nations. You are here, giving your attention to the Open Secret. And there is a reason.

Before you got here, you probably read the invitation on our website or iBooks or Amazon. You read "*... describes the ecstatic art of Awakening Coaching: how anyone can be a support to anyone else in discovering the Open Secret that is an infinite source of stillness, well-being, and creativity, and bringing it forth in every area of their life.*" There was something about one or more of those words that made you want to explore this right now, more than bungee jumping while knitting small kitten hats. What was it?

Imagine for a moment that you are walking on a busy street in a small town you are visiting. You pass the travel agency and see posters in the window for Corfu, or Hawaii, or the Grand Canyon. You hardly notice, and you walk on by. Then you pass the flower shop. Bright yellow tulips, flown in from Holland. Orchids. A dozen red roses, going for a deal. But they do not move you, and you walk on by. Then you pass the clothing store. "50% off—latest colors and fashions." Sweaters, pants, hats, shoes. Yes, shoes! All kinds and colors and sizes of beautiful, sexy, sophisticated, and on-sale shoes. But again, you walk on by, hardly noticing.

And then you come to a restaurant. You can smell the aroma of the food wafting out onto the street. You hardly notice what kind of restaurant it is, you hardly glance at the menu once you get seated, and you eagerly order the first thing you see.

Why?

Why were the flower shop and the travel agent and the clothing store all uninteresting, but the restaurant drew you right in, with only a minimal glance at the menu? You already know the answer. It is because you were hungry, right? If you are hungry enough you do not even care about the decor, or the customer reviews on *Yelp*, or whether the salad was locally grown. If you are hungry enough, you just want to eat, and as quickly as possible.

There is also another kind of hunger. It is not a hunger for food, or a thirst for liquid, or even a desire for anything tangible at all. I like to call it by a different word, to make the distinction clear. I call it *longing*. In my language, desire is for something that you have already defined in your mind. "I want more money." That is clear. Take some action, and maybe eventually you get the money. But there is still desire, for even more, or for something different. "I want to be in a relationship. I'm so lonely, I want to find the Right One." In the same way, either you keep on desiring, from one dating site to another, or you find someone to be in relationship with. But almost always, after a few months, the desire changes. "I want my partner to be different, to be more caring, more available, more like

I wanted in the first place." And then a little later another desire appears, "I want to be alone."

> *I want chocolate.*
> *I want my free upgrade.*
> *I want a BMW.*
> *I want to be famous.*
> *I want to be a rock star.*
> *I want to be powerful.*
> *I want to rule the whole world.*

All of these desires lead to more desires. But longing is different. It can be very, very strong, it can eclipse the interest for anything else in your life, but we do not necessarily know, clearly and logically, what the longing is for.

The Longing for Home

Let me tell you a little story.

Fred goes shopping at Costco. Just like everyone else, he shows his membership card, gets himself a shopping cart, and begins to wander among stacks of TVs, tools, clothes, food, and books. But then Fred is a little careless, and he runs his cart into a huge display of basketballs, each in its own box. The whole thing comes crashing down on top of Fred, and he is thrown to the floor. For a few moments our intrepid hero is knocked unconscious. People come to rescue him from under the pile, and he soon comes around, with a sore bump on the back of his head.

Fred is fine, except that he cannot remember where he is, who he is, what his name is, or what he is supposed to be doing in this strange place.

Fred sits up. He looks around. "What kind of place is this?" he asks himself. He sees people, almost all of them in a hurry, pushing carts down aisles, looking to the left and right, and taking things from the shelves.

> *"Batteries. I want more for me."*
>
> *"Five-pound bucket of guacamole. I want that for me."*
>
> *"Jeans. Give me five pairs. Five for me."*
>
> *"Shampoo. A gallon for me. More, more, more, I want more for me."*

Fred also sees other busy people, dressed in white coats, some driving forklifts, putting more things onto the shelves.

"Where am I?" Fred asks himself, rubbing his head. "What is this place?" He struggles to his feet; he steadies himself on his shopping cart. Fred wants to fit in, so he also starts to walk down the aisles. Somewhat mechanically, he also starts to take things from the shelves and put them in his cart. When in Rome, do as the Romans do. But inside himself, there is a small voice. "*I want to go home,*" the voice whispers. "*I don't really like this place so much. I don't mind the TVs or the food or the books or the clothes. It all looks very nice. And useful. But everyone is in such a hurry. I want to go home.*"

The problem for Fred is that he has lost his memory. He cannot remember where home is, or what home is. He just knows that home is not this place. He has an intuition, a memory in his cells, that home is peaceful, home is relaxed, home is comfortable, home is familiar. He knows that at home he needs nothing, he is missing nothing. At home his cart is always already full.

Gradually, Fred is taken over by this longing, this yearning for something that his mind cannot remember or describe, but his heart cannot forget. It haunts him. "*I want to go home so much. I am tired. I want to rest where I belong. I want to go home so badly, but I don't remember the address, the street, even the area of town.*" Fred is deeply, painfully homesick.

Is there anything about that story that feels familiar to you? Do you ever feel this same way, living here on planet Earth? Just like Fred? Do you sometimes step back and look at everyone rushing into their future, that same rush in which you get caught as well, and feel homesick, even though you may not consciously remember home at all? Once it takes hold of you, this longing can be confusing and disorienting. It will not let you alone; it will no longer allow you to get fully immersed in the feeding frenzy. Yet at the same time it is vague, it is undefined.

It is this feeling of vague longing that leads Fred to Aisle 387, where they keep the self-help books and CDs, the DVDs, and the tickets for seminars and retreats. Because Fred feels such a deep longing, and because he has lost his memory and cannot remember his home, he feels very attracted to all of this merchandise. He loads up his cart with many things. Fred may find a teacher, or a teaching, or even several that appeal to him. He may discover maps and concepts about where home is, and how to get there. He may join groups, and learn a new vocabulary and way of behaving. He may find fellow travelers on the path home. Fred may create a brand new identity as a "seeker," and start to feel more comfortable with others who feel the same way.

But even after all this, Fred discovers that the feeling of longing still remains. It may become dampened by these theories, and maps, and fellow travelers. Fred may start to feel more at ease. But still the longing for home is there.

Have you also been shopping on Aisle 387? Have you found maps to follow; concepts about your peak potential, about "Enlightenment" and ultimate reality? Have you ever fallen in love with a charismatic teacher? Have you sometimes found a group to be part of, and belong to? And have you also found that all of those things may leave the longing for home just as strong, in the innermost part of you?

Follow the Longing

There have always been a few people, in every culture, in every age, who followed this longing back into themselves with enough passion that they found their way home. They found the Open Secret beyond the mind, beyond the endless procession of thoughts and feelings, beyond the automatic machinery of desire. These people became the peak of what we see as possible for a human being. Buddha, Jesus, Lao Tzu, Thomas Jefferson, Albert Einstein, William Blake, Michelangelo ... Britney Spears (just checking if you are paying attention). Today there are millions of people who have tapped into the Open Secret that makes everything sparkle. They may have found it only in snapshots, or they may have found it in more sustained ways. I have interviewed hundreds of people who have shifted their consciousness in this way, and who are now leading creative lives, overflowing with contribution, making a huge difference to the world. Here is the single most important thing I can tell you about these people:

Many of them had a teacher, or even many teachers, at one time or another. Many did not. Some were part of a group, read books, and went on retreats. Many did not. Some were vegetarian, or did yoga or meditation. And many did not. Some wore Birkenstocks, ate granola, and got Om tattoos. Most did not. What every single one had in common, without exception, was that they found a way to follow their natural longing. Getting in touch with this longing, and following it home, is the single key that works every time. It may lead you to peaks of worldly triumph, it may lead you through valleys of grief and despair, but it will always bring you all the way to the Open Secret that is your true home.

Did the restaurant give you the hunger? Of course not. The hunger was already there. It was in you before the restaurant appeared, and it was the hunger that made the restaurant interesting. The hunger is yours; it comes from you. It is not learned, or imitated, or conditioned.

It is very, very important to see this. To claim this. To own this. It is the difference between being a walk-on extra in someone else's movie and being the star of your own adventure.

The feeling of "I want to go home" was not given to you by any teacher or teaching. You did not get it from any book or CD, and you did not learn it from any seminar. It is yours. It was this longing, already alive within you, that made all of these things attractive. It is because of this longing, whether it is a flicker or a fireworks display, that you are interested in what I may have to say to you today.

Now, truthfully, not everyone on the planet has this sense of longing alive in them for the Open Secret. Many human beings are not really interested in this longing at all. It has been too deeply buried. Their primary interest is in accumulating money, driving the fastest car, having more power, and more sex, with more people, in more unusual positions. There is nothing wrong with any of those things. We can all live this life however we want to. But once the longing takes hold, it becomes important to attend to it carefully. It demands that from us.

I have been guiding people into the rediscovery of this Open Secret since 1991. I have worked with hundreds of people individually, and tens of thousands of people in seminars and groups. I have trained more than 1,300 people in how to become facilitators of the Open Secret themselves. In every case, for any of this to have any real impact, we have to awaken this longing, and give it expression. If we approach it in this way, then this conversation is serving you, and you do not need to serve or follow anything outside yourself.

Try it for Yourself

So let us start here. Please put everything aside for just a few minutes and ask yourself this vitally important question:

What is my deepest longing?

Don't think about it too much. Write the question at the top of a piece of paper, and then just let rip. Write as many answers as come to you spontaneously in five minutes, and then let us pick up again.

What is my Deepest Longing?

1 _____

2 _____

3 _____

4 _____

5 _____

6 _____

7 _____

8 _____

9 _____

10 _____

11 _____

12 _____

13 _____

14 _____

All done? Great. I would be interested to hear what your answers were. You can type them in the readers' website we have created for you.[3] I have asked this question of thousands of people from all over the world. I ask it at the beginning of every session with every new coaching client. I ask it at the start of every weekend seminar, from Maui to Munich to Memphis. And I ask this question of everyone at the start of every course to train new Awakening Coaches. This question is the beginning of Awakening Coaching.

It is a different question from *"What do you want?"* See the difference? *"What is your desire?"* asks: as you have been walking down the aisles with your shopping cart, what are the things you have been taking from the shelves? *"What is your deepest longing?"* asks: what is that deeper whisper that is not wanting any thing at all, but that reminds you of the sense of home?

Here are the most frequent answers I hear from people. Please check them out and compare them with your own.

My Deepest Longing is for:

> *Peace.*
> *Stillness.*
> *Freedom from the mind.*
> *Finding my unique gift.*
> *Love without fear.*
> *An end to worrying.*
> *Opening my heart.*
> *Doing boldly what I came here for.*
> *Belonging.*
> *Loving deeply.*

---

[3] http://better-than-sex.kajabi.com/groups/9765

Let me Serve You

In this book I am going to show you how to bring this longing alive, and how to follow it all the way home to the Open Secret that is your true nature. I am going to show you ways to live your day-to-day life in a way that honors the Open Secret. And, if you are interested, I am going to show you how you can become a support to anyone else to do the same.

I am not a teacher, or a guru, or a philosopher. I am not here to deliver a teaching, or give you anything, or tell you what you should do with your life. I do not represent any group or tradition. I am here in service to the hunger, to the longing, that is already in you. You have the longing. You have the hunger. I have a small restaurant. Nothing fancy. Just some rice, some vegetables, maybe a little chicken, some fish. A very simple restaurant. If you come with your hunger, I can honor it. That is my job. I am an Awakening Coach, and I train other people to become Awakening Coaches, too.

I want to talk with you now about what that means, and why these words are important. What is awakening? What is coaching? And what happens when you bring these words together? The best way to answer this question is for you to meet some of my friends here at the party. So c'mon down now, follow me to the basement, and I'll introduce you to some very interesting people.

CHAPTER 3

What is Awakening?

Come down with me now to the basement. Watch your head on the beam there. A few friends are down here, watching a movie together. I know, it smells a little musty down here. It got flooded during a storm a few years back and we never managed to get rid of the smell of the mold. Is it bothering you? I hope not. The TV down here is very old. The picture flickers a little bit, and perhaps you can also hear the low buzzing sound it makes.

See that man sitting on the sofa there, who looks a little like Matthew McConaughey? A few days' beard growth, faded jeans, with the very nice shoes? His name is Mark Thornton. The very beautiful woman sitting next to him is his wife, Charlotte. She is an actress from Sweden. Let me introduce you. Back in 1999, Mark was the Chief Operating Officer of J. P. Morgan Private Bank in London. Back then it was one of the biggest private banks in the world. He was earning a huge salary doing what investment bankers do: moving money around. One day, his life completely changed.

Here Mark, put that movie on pause for a moment; tell them the story yourself.

Sure, Arjuna. I was living in London. It was six-thirty in the morning in the summertime. I was standing on the subway platform heading to work. They call it "the Tube" in London. I was standing there in my shirt and tie with my briefcase, preoccupied as always with all the usual stresses and worries and concerns and mild panics of being the COO of an international bank.

And then, on that subway platform, there was a moment out of time. Suddenly, I was completely drawn out of all the thinking, the processing, the analyzing. I was in a state of openness and expansion that was completely and radically different from the identification with my own story and my very narrow to-do list for that day. It was such a completely unknown and unexpected shift that it was shocking, in a way. There was something in that moment that was so profoundly refreshing, so incredibly nurturing, and yet very simple, very direct.

Throughout the day the same thing kept happening. A door to something vast had opened, and I found I could return to it just by paying attention to it. I had heard about people having shifts in their state of consciousness. I had believed the popular myth that these shifts only happen to people who live in India, who have robes and white beards and dedicate their entire lives to spiritual seeking. And here I was, just an ordinary guy, standing on a subway platform, holding his briefcase. I was really intrigued.

Later that day, I was chairing a meeting of the Board of Directors of the bank. This is, as you can imagine, usually a fairly formal affair. I introduced the first speaker. And there was another pause. I found myself stepping back, away from my normal kind of contraction. I was back in the same incredible openness: an irrational sense of oneness with all the people in the room. Not only had my own sense of limitation dropped away completely, but I could feel everyone else there free of their personal contractions as well, in their natural innocence. My heart just exploded. There I was, sitting at the table with my meeting notes, chairing a meeting at a bank, and feeling an indescribable sense of connection, and humor, and play.

My life since that day has been devoted to exploring ways to live this same openness and freedom, so that my everyday life can actually support that awakening rather than close it down. I wanted to find out how my ordinary human life can be a real opportunity for this kind of awakening to start to spread, to flow, to influence the words I speak, to shift my energy and how I spend each day.

Thanks, Mark. My friend is describing a moment of awakening. In the last couple of decades the same kind of shift has happened for millions of people. Limits drop away, and you find yourself returning to your natural state of consciousness, without the usual sense of separation, and without stress. I first met Mark in 1999, soon after his first moment of awakening. He resigned from his job at the bank in 2001, and soon after that he took the training to become an Awakening Coach. Since then, he has been coaching bankers and executives in how to bring awakening into the workplace. Find out more about Mark here: markthornton.us[4]

Awakening is the simplest thing we could possibly think about or talk about. If we prefer it to be complex, that can also be arranged quite easily. We can put many esoteric theories around it, we can twirl chakras, we can battle through barriers of karma and dogma, and past lives and loves, and, hey presto, we have made it complicated. But the essence of awakening is incredibly simple.

Zooming Out

The movie that Mark and Charlotte and the others have returned to watching is, coincidentally, called *Awakenings*. It is based on a true story by Oliver Sacks, about a group of patients in a mental hospital who all suffer from a kind of catatonic trance state. They can eat and drink (often with help) but they cannot interact normally with the world. Dr. Sayer, a young psychiatrist played by Robin Williams, has been successful in reversing their symptoms by using an experimental drug. They all come alive again, able to enjoy their lives, to laugh and sing and give their gifts. One of these patients, named Leonard, played by Robert De Niro, is in his early twenties. His symptoms took over when he was still a boy.

---

[4] http://markthornton.us/

In the scene you are watching now, Dr. Sayer is just arriving at the hospital in the middle of the night. Leonard had got into the doctor's office and used the phone to ask him to come over urgently. The doctor walks into his office and sees Leonard sitting at the desk.

"Sit down," says Leonard. "We've got to tell everybody," he goes on. He is waving his hands, highly animated and passionate. "We've got to remind them how good it is…."

"How good what is, Leonard?" the doctor asks.

Leonard picks up the newspaper. "Read it," he says. "It's all bad. It's all bad. People have forgotten what life is all about. What it is to be alive. They need to be reminded. They need to be reminded of what they have, and what they can lose. What I feel is the joy of life. The gift of life. The freedom of life." He is shaking his hands in the air and grinning. "The wonderment of life…."

Now Charlotte pauses the movie again. The buzzing from the TV has become worse and they are trying to fix it. Now where is Leonard? Where is Dr. Sayer? Where is the whole dramatic tension of whether the drug will work? Dr. Sayer's challenge, the sadness of Leonard's condition: these problems have not been solved; they have been dissolved with one click of the remote.

But wait. We are also not really in the basement of my house, are we? I made it up, as a device to write this book for you, as a way to invite you into the book. There is no mold in my basement. I don't even have a basement. There is no TV in this basement that does not exist, and my good friends Mark and Charlotte have never sat on the couch that does not exist in the non-existent basement. There is no mold, no buzz. These problems have been dissolved; they do not require any solution.

In fact I am sitting in my house, at my desk, with my laptop in front of me. If I look up for a moment I see the trees outside the window. It is fall as I write this, and I can see every shade of green, golden brown, and even reds and darker browns in the trees. I can see the letters appearing on the white screen as I type.

What can you see where you are? You are seeing these letters on a white page. If you look up from the book or the screen, do you notice colors, and textures, and the size of things? All day long, every day, we are seeing countless shapes and colors and movements and textures.

I can hear the sound of the heated air blowing into the living room. I can also hear the sound of the tapping of the keys as I type this for you. From outside the window I can hear the sound of a distant motor somewhere. It might be traffic.

Now you listen. What sounds can you hear where you are? Label them to yourself, by saying "I hear music" or "I hear a car." All day long, every day, we are hearing countless sounds, dancing and layering on top of each other. In fact it is very rarely, and perhaps never, totally silent.

What sensations can you feel in your body just now? In the same way, label them by saying to yourself, "I feel my tongue in my mouth," "I feel my feet touching each other," "I feel a soreness in my eyes." All day, every day, you and I and everyone we know are experiencing physical sensations. As long as you are awake, there are always a lot of exciting things to pay attention to in your body, now, and now, and now.

We could ask these same questions to anyone, anytime, anywhere on the planet, and almost everyone can find the answers. Besides a very small percentage who are blind or deaf, everyone is hearing, and seeing, and feeling. The content may change from one person to another. Some people may be seeing a 55,000-square-foot mansion with a yacht outside in the bay; others may be seeing the prison cell they share with five other inmates. The perceived quality of what you are seeing may change, but what is common to everybody is that we are all having sensory-based experience.

Secondary Reality

There is also another layer of experience happening for us all the time. In addition to hearing sounds, seeing color and movement, and feeling sensations, there is a secondary layer that is created in thought. These thoughts are rarely about what is happening now; they mostly run into the past and into the future, and they are mostly out of control.

This secondary layer, as far as we know, is special to human beings. When you see your dog sitting out on the porch in the evening, do you suppose that the dog is thinking about how to create a better future? It seems unlikely. Do fleas regret past actions, or use the law of attraction to hit the mother-lode-of-all-veins?

This capacity to create experience in thought is, of course, both a blessing and a curse. It allows an architect to imagine an elaborate building in thought, draw the plans, and pass them on to a company that can construct the building. It allows us to create great art and literature, to imagine and invent so many things.

This secondary layer becomes a curse, very simply, when we can no longer unplug from it. Our capacity to create images of what is not actually here makes a fantastic servant, but a catastrophic master. The mechanisms of comparison, judgment, concern for the future, and regret for the past can all be useful in small doses as a conscious choice. But for almost everyone, the thinking process has gone berserk, and has eclipsed our capacity to experience what is real in this moment. Just a tiny trickle of attention is left for what we can hear and see and feel, and the larger part of our attention is, almost all of the time, lost in thought. Just like Leonard, we are also in a kind of trance state. We have lost the wonderment of life.

Once trapped in this very limited movie, the best we can do is to try to change negative and limiting thoughts into positive ones. We try to shift fear into optimism, control into acceptance, and desire into gratitude. This is the massive industry of affirmations and positive thinking. But how does it work out? The majority of people report that these limited and negative thoughts keep coming back, again and again and again. In fact they have to, because the sense of being small and separate will keep generating a sense of fear and impending danger. Even when we are successful at changing limiting thoughts into their more expansive and positive cousins, we still find ourselves trapped in a prison of limitation, only now with more attractive wallpaper.

Find the "I"

Awakening is not like that. It is not about changing the content of your experience in any way at all, or even about trying to change your thoughts. Awakening means simply to recognize the Open Secret that is experiencing all of this.

In this moment you are hearing sounds, correct? You are seeing the color and shape and size of things. It is also possible to notice thoughts passing. You say "I hear the sound," "I see the movement," "I was aware of the thought." What is this "I"?

All day long we say "I" and "me" and "my." "*I want to go to the movies. I am bored. I love you. Look at me. Leave me alone. This is my body, my car, my children, my relationship.*" But we do not really know what this "I" is. When we try to find it, we generally end up telling a story about the past. None of that story can be experienced now, except as thoughts.

We meet each other and exchange stories. Whoever you are, whatever your story is, thoughts will rush in to fill the vacuum and tell the story, but who is aware of those thoughts? Who is aware of the story itself? The story is made up of thoughts and memories. None of them explain the mystery of who or what is hearing the sounds, seeing the movement, and noticing the thoughts in this moment.

In fact, we all live in a kind of hypnosis. When we hear a sound, our attention is so completely kidnapped by the content of our experience that there is only the sound, no awareness of that which is hearing it. The same is true of seeing and feeling. When thoughts pass, the content of the thought takes us over so completely that we lose any sense of who is aware of the thoughts.

Awakening is simple. It is a moment of recognition where the attention really, deeply, profoundly shifts from this churning of identifying with thoughts, and feelings, and history, and story, and likes, and dislikes, to finding out who is actually aware of this moment. This recognition may happen just for a split second, and in fact it does all the time: at the peak of orgasm, during extreme sports, in the gap between being awake and falling asleep, we are always touching into this infinite realm beyond the mind. It might also be sustained for a few minutes at a time, or even hours or days. And it may become a constantly accessible undercurrent to everything else that is occurring.

Even the tiniest taste of this is life-changing.

The Concept is not IT

As you read the words on these pages, you are reading concepts about awakening. But the concepts are not at all the same thing as the direct recognition of awakening itself. In just the same way, when you are very hungry, reading a book about nutrition and digestion may be interesting and informative, but it can never begin to satisfy your hunger. When you feel horny, reading or understanding about the hormones that generate sexual desire may be fascinating, but it will never, ever, come close to great lovemaking. Awakening means that the attention comes fully into recognition of itself. It means to recognize, in a moment of "Aha!," that which has always been here, seeing movement, feeling sensations, hearing sounds.

That can never be something you have to work towards in the future, because it is already here. It is that which is already experiencing everything else, now, and now, and now. When Jesus had this awakening, he realized that "I and the

Father are One." When Buddha had this awakening, he realized that "I am not just Siddhartha the Prince. I am Buddha. I am awareness."

Until recently, the few people, here and there, who tasted this were often men, and also frequently monks or recluses. In the last few decades, all of that has changed. When I started to point people's attention to this, in 1991, there were very few people who had direct awakening for themselves. Most came for a "contact high" from someone else who had already tasted it. Today, when I travel and teach weekend seminars, or work with coaching clients one-on-one over the phone, everyone, and I mean EVERYONE, is dropping into this awakening for real, on the first morning or in the first coaching session. Many of my friends are also guiding people in this way: Jean Houston, Eckhart Tolle, Adyashanti, Richard Moss. They all report from the road a massive explosion of direct awakening, at least in moments. The secret is out.

What's the Big Deal?

This kind of shift of consciousness can have huge consequences for your day-to-day life. Historically, it was often separated from life, and so became the territory of monks, nuns, and recluses. But once we let go of this artificial compartmentalization, we discover that awakening to your deepest nature can in fact be the perfect fertilizer that makes every aspect of your life blossom and bloom. Here are just a few of the amazing and glorious ways that awakening can light up your Christmas tree.

Peace. Everything we experience through our senses, as well as every fleeting thought and feeling, is constantly shifting and changing. It is all subject to birth and death. When we are glued to this world of changing things, it is like being on a roller coaster that never, ever, stops. Just a moment of awakening returns you to that which does not change. Awareness is a constant. Hence you are flooded with peace, with stillness, with a feeling of coming home.

Feeling Good for no Reason. These moments of touching into stillness have a very powerful impact on the body. So much of our energy is generally caught up in worry and protecting ourselves from a world that we feel separate from. We live in bodies that are riddled with tension and stress. Awakening is the ultimate stress-buster. As soon as you relax into who you truly are, even for a moment, there is a rush of well-being released in the belly and the heart. It spreads in waves through the rest of the body.

It was in this immersion into euphoria that the title of this book was born. A student in one of my trainings was struggling to describe this powerful feeling of bliss though her whole body that often accompanies a taste of awakening, and she finally grinned, "It's better than sex!" I liked that phrase and told her it would make a great book title.

The Oneness Hidden beneath Separation. Awakening can, if we allow it to, have a very sweet impact on our intimate relationships. When you meet another person, whether your husband, or wife, or boyfriend, or girlfriend, or child, or mother, or father, or friend, if you are glued to thoughts and feelings, the sense of separation will be inevitable. Awakening returns you to the dimension of you that is not separate. The awareness that hears and sees and feels is still; it is silent and infinite and has no boundaries. Quickly, we discover it is the same awareness that is experiencing all this in you and me and everyone we know. We come to discover that love is not actually an emotion you feel, but the recognition that your own true nature and the true nature of the other are the same.

The Solution to Every Problem. Thought is generated from the sense of a separate me that feels threatened, weak, and vulnerable, so it easily becomes combative. Awakening allows us to experience life from an expansive state of consciousness that is relaxed and humorous, and that knows creativity and solutions. Albert Einstein once said, "You cannot solve any problem in the same state of consciousness in which it was created." You now know how to relax into a more expansive dimension of yourself in which solutions naturally bubble up on their own.

Your Unique Gift. In my life, I have been fortunate enough to meet a few totally happy and fulfilled people. These are people who not only have experienced powerful moments of awakening, but have also awoken to a unique gift that wanted to flow through them. Lynne Twist, for example, has raised more than two billion dollars to alleviate world hunger. John Gray, after spending nine years in a meditation center in Switzerland focusing only on awakening, went on write the most popular book about intimate relationship in all of history. Awakening can also allow you to uncover the unique gift that is waiting inside of you, and to discover how to share it with the world.

This is not a matter of religious belief or philosophy, and requires no change of lifestyle, so we might ask ourselves why so many people live their lives in any other way. The answer lies in the way that awakening has generally been spread, which has often been hierarchical and patriarchal. In just the last few decades a new model has emerged that allows us to explore awakening in a radically new way.

CHAPTER 4

What is Coaching?

I want to introduce you to another extraordinary friend, someone who, just like Mark, was in the right place at the right time to be part of another leap in human evolution. Come over here and meet Dave Buck, who worked side-by-side for many years with Thomas J. Leonard, widely considered to be the founder of modern-day coaching. With Leonard, Dave created CoachVille, the largest organization to train coaches in the world, and is still today the main teacher and CEO.

We may have become a little blasé about coaching in the last few years. There are so many kinds of coaches today: wellness coaches, executive coaches, find-your-mate coaches, relationship coaches, divorce coaches, find-the-right-coach coaches. Sometimes when I go to conferences or parties it seems that there are a lot more coaches than clients! So we may need to remind ourselves now and then what a delicious, beautiful, respectful, and inspiring relationship coaching represents. It can give us renewed optimism about the possibilities of human potential.

It Started with Sports

Just twenty or thirty years ago we found coaching in only one area of life: sports. Back then we had tennis coaches, swimming coaches, basketball coaches, and football coaches. The coach would enter into a relationship with an athlete or a team to bring forth their greatest potential, and to help them reach goals that neither of them could otherwise reach on their own. Coaching is the ultimate collaborative relationship. Before he worked in life coaching, Dave was already a football coach for his local team. In working with Thomas J. Leonard, they recognized together that it was essentially collaboration that was at the heart of the next step in human evolution. Here is Dave:

> *I always like to talk about the Olympics: they bring the whole world together. The Olympics in China were watched by 4.7 billion people, more than half the human beings on Planet Earth. It is a global phenomenon. There is something about the pursuit of human greatness that touches us so deeply we will take any opportunity to see it on display. On the TV, they spend almost as much screen time showing the coach as they do the athlete. It accentuates the fact that this expression of excellence does not only involve the athletes: they also have this other person in their life.*

> *How do we bring that pursuit of human greatness to all areas of life, not just in athletics? You can pursue human greatness in leadership, in relationship, in being the mayor of your small town, in being an entrepreneur with a small company. It is that pursuit that unifies our humanness: raising the bar together on what is possible for humanity. People of all endeavors of life want to pursue human greatness in their own way. I believe humanity is at a place now where we want to evolve and we want to bring human greatness to all aspects of life, to pursue mastery, enjoy life, and play as big as we can possibly play. That is what is causing the coaching phenomenon.*

It is worth pausing to consider the miraculous and revolutionary implications of what Dave is talking about: to migrate the coaching relationship from sports to other fields. Take Michael Phelps, for example, who has been coached by Bob Bowman since he was eleven years old. Phelps has won eighteen Olympic gold medals, more than any other athlete in history. He often says that he owes his success as a swimmer to Bowman: *"Training with Bob is the smartest thing I've ever done.... I'm not going to swim for anyone else."* Bowman has never won a gold medal. He swam for a team (the Seminoles) for a couple of years in the early 80s, but otherwise his entire career has been in coaching others to be great swimmers. Bowman's extraordinary gift is not primarily as an athlete, but in bringing out the hidden potential in others. For Phelps to win so many medals, these two men needed each other equally. Phelps says he could never have won any medal without his coach. And of course, Bowman needed Phelps in the same way.

This is a huge leap from the more hierarchical approach that has dominated education of every kind for as long as we can remember. Think, for example, of the great painter Michelangelo, known the world over for his paintings on the Sistine Chapel ceiling and his sculptures of David and the Pietà. He was apprenticed to Domenico Ghirlandaio when he was thirteen years old. This was customary at the time. The boy washed brushes, prepared walls with whitewash for frescos, and cleaned up at the end of the day. Ghirlandaio was the Master, and Michelangelo was the student. It was expected that the relationship would respect the Master, and that the needs or talent of the student would be next to irrelevant. In fact, when Michelangelo rebelled against this relationship it created great conflict, and the apprenticeship was over within a few months.

Coaching is the opposite of an apprenticeship like that. The coach can say, "I am simply in service to your brilliance. What is important here is not my brilliance, but yours." That is coaching. And that is fantastic! It is the antidote to hierarchy and patriarchy, which have dominated our planet for five thousand years. The coach is a friend, standing by your side, seeing your brilliance and working to bring it forth.

The Development of Modern Coaching

Back in 1974, Timothy Gallwey wrote a game-changing (literally!) book called *The Inner Game of Tennis*. Many people consider this book the first step from the sports coaching model towards personal coaching. The book was based on humanistic and transpersonal psychological principles, and "the concept that the opponent within is more formidable than the one outside."

Many years later, Gallwey was in San Francisco, engaged in an extraordinary conversation with Werner Erhard and Stewart Emery, who were in the process of developing the est Training, and Michael Murphy, co-founder of the Esalen Institute. Together they were beginning to explore how we can create an environment where people can thrive; where they can be guided without being controlled. How can you guide someone to become resourceful and creative?

Thomas J. Leonard was the accountant at the est Training. So he was privy to this exploration, without being directly involved initially. It was Leonard who took that conversation from a new kind of relationship to defining a new career, which people could be trained in and earn an income from. Dave Buck remembers:

> *Thomas would say, "I love this idea of guiding and helping people be successful and sharing what I've learned, but also challenging people to find their own answers and be creative and self-expressed." He made it a job. He made it an economically viable profession. It was always something people did out of love, but there was no economical way to do it. And that's why he's seen as the father of life coaching .*

Leonard went on to found the International Coach Federation, which is now the global body that is advancing coaching as a profession worldwide. He also founded Coach University, the first professional coaching school. Here's Dave Buck again:

> *Thomas was a force of nature. He had a determination that he was going to create a new profession, recognized all over the world, and nothing would stop him. After we first got to know each other in 1997, I spoke to him every day on the phone until he died. He was training people to be collaborative, and he was extraordinarily collaborative himself. The*

way that he made this coaching thing happen in the world was that he was always getting people together, whoever was interested in his idea, in face-to-face meetings, or in teleconferences. He had this idea called the "research and development team." Every time we wanted to create a program, he would send an email out to everyone saying, "I'm going to have a call on Friday to work on this idea. If you want to work on it, join the call."

He was this amazing collaborator and synthesizer. He would pull ideas from people from different walks of life to create this thing that is now called life coaching. It was really a remarkable experience.

Thomas J. Leonard is widely revered not only for creating a new profession, but as a consequence for changing the way we think about ourselves and our potential and how to realize it. One of the best short accounts of the development of coaching is by Bill Dueease, co-founder of The Coach Connection. No one has summed up Leonard's contribution better than this:

Thomas created a new human-improvement process that assisted people to discover and unravel the mystery of themselves. The greatest mystery in the world is not global warming, nor whether the Cubs will ever win the series, but ourselves. This new human-improvement process called personal coaching works exceptionally well to assist you to clearly, quickly, completely, and confidentially discover yourself, without any hint of judgment or guilt. With your personal coach, you will become the World's Leading Expert on you. The greatest form of human improvement and growth is self-awareness.

Today life coaching has become a well-respected profession worldwide. It has impacted almost every area of life that we can imagine. Let us remind ourselves of a few of the key things that are so amazing and revolutionary about coaching.

Six Reasons to Celebrate Coaching

Reason No. 1: Coaching is Respectful. A coach could say to an athlete, "I am not as good a player as you. I could never do what you can do. I see your potential. I believe in your potential. I know what is possible for you. I will stay by your side. I will encourage you, even when you feel like giving up, to bring forth your ability to go as far as you can go." The coach looks deeply into the player with the clear eyes of absolute respect. He or she sees the potential and calls that forth.

Whether in sports or any other area of life, the coach is saying, "Don't worry about me at all. Don't even look at me. Look into yourself and your potential. Become the ultimate that you can be."

Dave Buck comments:

> If you're going to coach swimming, you should know swimming, you should have been a swimmer. But you don't have to be a world-class swimmer to coach someone to become one. You don't have to have been the greatest in the world to coach someone to be the greatest in the world.

Reason No. 2: Coaching is Facilitating our Evolution beyond Hierarchy. In almost every field of life, we have been used to learning from a master as a student or a disciple. It is how most of us went to school, how many of us were parented, how we learned music, and sports, and languages, and even relationship and sexuality.

"But Mom, why do I have to clean my room / go to bed / read this book / eat this spinach?"

"Because I say so. That's why."

End of conversation.

The coach is not a teacher or a master. Nor is the coach a servant. The coach is a profound and deep well-wisher, standing by your side, sensing your innate brilliance and bringing it forth. This is the most empowering relationship you can imagine.

Dave comments again:

> *Coaching is a collaborative relationship. It's not just "my way or the highway." The coach must be able to share ideas and wisdom and a game plan and thoughts and strategies. Not because the player has to do it that way, but so the player can take what the coach is sharing, blend it with their own unique ideas, and use that co-creation to bring about a new possibility. You are correct to say that it is not hierarchical, not from a lack of expertise, but because it works better in collaboration. People become great not when someone tells them what to do, but when someone guides them to try out ideas that they can then coalesce into their own vision.*

Reason No. 3: Coaching is Client-Centered. As we will soon see with Awakening Coaching, as well as every other kind of coaching, Leonard's legacy is all about asking powerful questions. There is an underlying assumption in any coaching relationship that, deep down, the client is resourceful, that everything the client is aspiring to is already within them. The client has an intuition of their true potential. The client has a sense of the habits and beliefs that get in the way. And the client also often has a sense of the simplest and quickest way forward. The coach knows how to ask the right questions to bring this forth, to actualize it. Dave Buck reminds us of the evolutionary process we have collectively passed through in this way:

> *The Industrial Age created the idea that human beings are like buckets: they don't know anything and they need to be filled, told exactly what to*

do and how to do it, so they can get it right the first time and never make any mistakes. Maslow and Carl Rogers developed humanistic psychology as an antidote: they felt that people had become hollow, just waiting for someone to tell them what to do. They saw this as disastrous for humanity. So they took the pendulum all the way to the other side, saying that people have all their own answers. You don't have to tell them what to do: they can figure everything out for themselves.

But now we know that both approaches are limited on their own. Sometimes we have a great idea within ourselves, and sometimes we don't have a damn idea what to do and we are grateful for someone who has experience to share with us.

Human beings are at their best when they collaborate, when they co-create. So a coach asks powerful questions. We love to share with others what we have learned. The key is to be able to do this in a way that doesn't dominate the other person. We are evolving to this new coaching way, which is always a collaboration.

Reason No. 4: Coaching is not about Dogma. Bowman did not attempt to teach Michael Phelps the Bowman Swimming Method, and then have him duplicate the approach. He could see that Phelps' long thin torso offered low drag, while his arms spanned six feet seven inches and could act as paddles to thrust him faster through the water. Bowman saw the young man's potential and then applied everything he knew about swimming to bring that potential forth. A great coach is highly skilled in a method of coaching that will bring forth the potential of the client, but that method is always in service to the client's brilliance and potential. In our case, for example, Awakening Coaching is a very precise method, which can be taught and learned and successfully duplicated. But it is never dogmatic: it is always secondary to the client's own experience, intuition, and wisdom.

Dave Buck comments:

> *A great coach typically has a method, and then personalizes with a player how to apply that method to the unique situation. Often a method is a great place to start, to learn basic skills, to get a level of success, to learn a love for the game. But then to go to real greatness you have to transcend the method. That is what great coaches do.*
>
> *This makes coaching very different from what we often call "self-help." The whole self-help movement was about "I did it this way, it worked for me, it should work for you, too." I believe the self-help movement has done more harm to humanity than just about anything else. Because if you read a self-help book and that author's method doesn't work for you, you can feel like a failure. That's just a disastrous, unintended consequence of the self-help movement. Coaching is the antidote to that.*

Reason No. 5: Coaching is Solution-Oriented. There are many other ways to work on our potential that focus on fixing what is wrong with us. We can always find layers of neurotic childhood conditioning; of dysfunctional beliefs and habits that can cause us to feel that the path to giving our gifts could be long and perilous, perhaps even hopeless. A good coach focuses on what is right with you, what is working for you, and builds on that. The coach assumes that you have a gift to give, a brilliance that wants to shine through you, and assists you to define it, play with it, and accentuate it so much that all that appears to be in your way disappears.

Reason No. 6: Coaching is about Play. Finally, because coaching comes from sports, it carries a sense of play into all areas of life. Play is lighthearted, and it reminds us of our childlike innocence. When we bring this notion of play to business, to leadership, to the very serious world of spiritual awakening, it is revolutionary. Dave Buck comments:

As we move out of the 20th-century Industrial Age of work and compliance and control, into this new age that I call the creative age of play, everything is about engagement and inspiration. Coaching people is becoming the leadership technology of the 21st century. Coaching is many things: it is transformational, it is empowering; but ultimately coaching is about helping someone play better, whatever their game is. When you play, you are fully engaged in the present moment. This is an amazing time in the world: we are shifting our focus from working and being goal-oriented to playing and being creative and self-expressed and engaged and fully present. That is what it takes to be successful now.

Coaching is an Evolving Discipline

Dave Buck points out that the coaching relationship is both a reflection of the environment in which it is created and a formative influence on that environment.

Earlier, in the 20th century, coaching often meant telling someone what to do in the right way, so they could get it right. Coaching had to evolve, even athletic coaching. Now we see coaches described in more collaborative terms. They are "working with the players" to come up with the game plan, rather than dictating the game plan. They are "working with the players" to find the best way to express their talent, rather than dictating how to express their talent. Coaching is about human performance, about playing better, and that is why it is so compelling. It is possible for coaching to evolve rapidly, because it is such a new field. It is able to evolve with how humans are ready to evolve.

Dave and Thomas were in dialog about the evolution of coaching from a sports model to other areas of life in the late 1990s and until 2003. Sadly,

Thomas J. Leonard died at the early age of 47. During his very short career he was able to apply collaborative coaching principles to business leadership, to education, to wellness, and to relationship skills. Many of these areas were deeply transformed from a top-down hierarchical approach to a new way that is more collaborative.

Leonard died before he was able to turn his attention to the area of life that has perhaps been more dominated by hierarchy and patriarchy than any other: the possibilities of spiritual awakening. Let us discover now what can happen when we bring coaching and awakening together, and meet a couple of real-life coaches who have explored this combination in their work with clients.

CHAPTER 5

What is Awakening Coaching?

Are you ready to meet some more of my friends? When we met Mark, we explored the essence of awakening, once it is liberated from the trappings of tradition and religion. We have talked about how awakening opens up a channel of creativity and well-being, beyond anything we could possibly create or imagine. When we met Dave Buck, we explored the miraculous relationship of coaching, which allows one person to support another; to recognize and bring forth hidden brilliance, free of any hierarchy. We also discovered how coaching is a relationship of humility and service.

Now I want to introduce you to two more of my friends, and we will discover the explosion of possibilities that opens up when we bring awakening and coaching together. This fusion fundamentally changes the context of awakening, and at the same time transforms the possibilities of coaching.

See those two beautiful women sitting on the couch together talking? They are both Awakening Coaches. Jeannie Campanelli is from Ontario, Canada, and she had a long background in more conventional coaching before she integrated awakening into her work. The woman she is sitting with is Satyaa Douglas, who was born in Germany, and now lives in Hawaii. Satyaa's whole life has been about the exploration of awakening. When she trained as a coach, she discovered how she could share her deepest awakening and passion with others. The two women have come to Awakening Coaching from opposite ends of the spectrum.

What Does Awakening Bring to Coaching?

When Jeannie trained to become an Awakening Coach, she had already been in professional practice as a coach for ten years. She had built her practice by specializing in supporting people to increase self-confidence. Here, Jeannie, you tell them in your own words:

> *There came a time when I realized that I wasn't going as deeply as I needed to in my work with self-confidence. I didn't have the tools, not only with other people, but also within myself, to be present with the critical mind, with all the old messages of not being good enough. So I started to search, because I knew I had to go deeper. That meant going below the surface of life, coming from the heart rather than what had been learned in the mind. Going deep meant entering the space of the core of us, the essential being in us.*
>
> *Bringing awakening into coaching opened a door for me to experience my own being-ness at another level. It opened the door for me to hold the space for my clients also to experience that vastness, that being-ness, that presence. I was able to touch into pure love, not conditional love, which is what I had known in my own experience. I was able to hold the space for that deeper love, at a whole new level. From that place of holding space for my clients, they also got to experience and expand that space within themselves. They had a new experience in the body about what it is like to live from a different place, beyond the thinking mind.*

This is the essential element that the integration of awakening brings to more conventional coaching. Instead of trying to fulfill the desires and alleviate the fears that the mind creates, the coach is able to drop deeper with the client, beyond the mind, beyond reactive feelings, and then everything shows up differently from that more expansive view. Instead of supporting the client to get what they think they want, it is now possible for the coach to support the client to relax into that deeper and more authentic longing. Here is Jeannie again:

> *Most of my clients were not feeling confident because they were run by unconscious core beliefs like "I'm not good enough" or "I'm not lovable." By learning many new tools, like Radical Awakening, I learned how to hold space for all my clients to experience deep inquiry.*

> *Can I now say that my clients are always self-confident? No! I learned to take the pressure off trying to be anything but who you are in this moment. The more they learn to accept the insecurity and self-doubt that arises—to observe it, to experience it, to be in it, and to see the pattern in it—the less it rules them. As they accept who they are in the moment, they are able to rest more deeply in natural presence and love, and to hold that space in their relationships. Less need shows up; fewer expectations or assumptions dominate their relationships, both personal and professional. They are much more at home in their own bodies, in their own skin, in who they naturally are, without having to change anything.*

I really do not have much to add to that: Jeannie just about said it all. When we add awakening to a coaching relationship, we shift from solving problems to dissolving them. When we experience beliefs and reactive feelings from that dimension, they seem like a mouse with a megaphone: lots of noise, but not much power. Many things clear up on their own, without any effort to try and fix them. Jeannie remembers one particular coaching client with whom she had already been working before she added these tools:

> *When I met her, she was in her late 20s, and had just started to do some IT consulting work with very large companies. She was something of a genius, very skilled and knowledgeable for her age. But she was just starting out a new career, and she was very shaky, very unconfident. When we started out we were focusing on problem-solving, reframing,*

helping her change her thinking. That was effective in helping her look at things in a different way. I was championing her to shift from limiting beliefs to expansive beliefs. But I also had the feeling that I was working on the surface, and there were deeper patterns at work, so it didn't stick very well. It was then that I knew I couldn't help her go deeper without going deeper myself.

I trained to be an Awakening Coach when she had already been my client for some months. I discovered this spaciousness, and silence, and stillness to be my own nature. I also discovered how easy it was to recognize and to take the resistance off core beliefs, so that they no longer ran my life. It opened the door for me. It has become my top priority.

When I got back from the training, I used these tools with her the very first week. I guided her right into Radical Awakening, and it was very easy for her.

She was a very practical business person, working with big companies, so I was actually surprised by how quickly, and how easily, she could have a direct realization of silence, and stillness, and spaciousness, how open she was to it, and how natural it was for her. If she had been presented with Buddhism or something Eastern, she might have rejected it; but since this relaxing into her natural state was done in a professional coaching context, she had nothing to resist. And she already trusted me.

I am still coaching her now. This spaciousness, this stillness, this openness has become something we return to in every session. Our coaching sessions happen now in the context of this spaciousness. There is more silence, and my own experience of spaciousness and silence has been a big part of that. I hold her in this.

I use a tool called Radical Releasing with her in every session. When she has limiting beliefs, instead of pushing them away, I have taught her to be in the energy of them, to be present in her body and be with them. She was a big fixer, a natural problem-solver. The art of problem-solving was perfect in her business, but it was not helpful when turned inward. She got to distinguish between the two. Now the patterns no longer drive her; she can watch them. She can be in them, and be OK with them, because now she knows that she is essentially much more than those patterns, much more than these feelings that come and go.

Now she runs her own company, she makes money so easily, and so many doors have opened in her life with major companies. She has become wealthy and successful beyond her wildest dreams.

Thank you, Jeannie. So many other professional coaches have found that their existing toolset blossomed and came alive once they knew how to access a limitless dimension of consciousness with their clients.

What Does Coaching Bring to Awakening?

Satyaa Douglas was born in northern Germany in 1962. When she finished high school she was prepared to study to be a psychotherapist or psychoanalyst.

I was longing for something deeper than I had come to know. I felt depressed by what I saw around me growing up: people living in a fear-based, survival paradigm, making choices out of fear. I felt that that kind of life was unacceptable; it was unbearable.

Before going to university, she took a year off, and traveled to India, where she wound up at the ashram of the controversial guru Bhagwan Rajneesh, later known as Osho.

My life changed: I felt like I had gone from hell to heaven. I felt that I was being bathed in unconditional love. It was something that I had been longing for, that I felt was really natural, but I had never experienced before. I became his student and he gave me my name. With him I realized how much I had been focused on myself, my thoughts and feelings and emotions. He saw the pure love at the core of everything. That changed my life around. I'm forever grateful for that glimpse that one person who had recognized love could pass to another.

After my year with Osho, I went back to Germany, where I had my place at university reserved. I went to school for one day, and I realized I wasn't going to go through with it. I realized that what I had been looking for I had already found while I was in India. So I took a leap and started traveling. I had many experiences. I had to live out my creative passions.

Satyaa's story is typical of many baby boomers who came of age in the late 60s and 70s. Many of us found gurus from India, Tibet, or China, and took on new names, new habits, and new values. Satyaa found Osho, something of a maverick, but many others found teachers who represented more established traditions.

For thousands of years, if someone felt this longing within themselves, and wanted support or encouragement, they would have had to find a priest or a guru. In most cases, in almost every culture and age, this would have been a man, and the context would have been hierarchical. Very often this required adopting a tradition, rules, beliefs, and restrictions on what you could eat, as well as your relationship to money and sex and a thousand other things. Getting support for the natural longing to awaken has, for the most part, come packaged with a pile of concepts and habits that may bear little relationship to the original longing.

But let's not throw out the baby with the bathwater. Having a teacher, being affiliated to a tradition, or studying ancient texts can all have many benefits. In Tibet, for example, the pursuit of awakening has been central to the culture for thousands of years, even before the arrival of Buddhism. You can learn practices such as *tonglen* or *gnondro*, knowing that they are not fresh out of the box, made up on the fly by a California New Age teacher hoping to make a quick buck. These tools have been thoroughly road-tested over countless generations. The bugs have been ironed out.

A real teacher can often see you better than you can see yourself. If the teacher really loves you and cares for you, he or she may see the ways in which you are tripping yourself up, again and again.

The teacher has already walked the journey, perhaps for many decades, and already knows the peaks and the valleys very well: what to avoid and what to embrace.

But there are also many important limitations to having a teacher, or affiliating oneself with a tradition.

If you assume that you must follow someone who is "Enlightened," to guide you out of your own sleep, the first problem is to discover someone who is actually qualified. There is no state license for gurus, no bar exam, and no professional organization of peers to keep members in line. There is no universal code of ethics.

Probably more than in any other area of life, signing up with a spiritual teacher is fraught with the risk of being taken advantage of: financially, or sexually, or just having your sense of energy and power sucked dry by "the mission." So many people in the last few decades have, out of their innocent longing for home, followed a teacher or a group to their own peril. I know so many people who have felt deeply disappointed and betrayed, and probably you do as well.

But perhaps the most important pitfall is that a traditional teacher–student relationship generally involves massive doses of projection. Out of our longing for home, for our natural state, and out of our inability to look within ourselves, we look for the perfect human being, who can do no wrong and make no mistakes. Satyaa remembers going to visit Rajneesh in Oregon, after he had left India:

> *I sat in a gathering and I noticed that when he left the stage, as excited as people had been while he was there, they fell back into being who they thought they were before. I felt like we were using him like a drug, to get a contact high: that we could see the love and the light in him but we hadn't truly turned it around and looked within. I remembered him saying, "I'm just a finger pointing to the moon; don't bite the finger." And I realized that this is what many of us were doing: biting the finger.*

Even if you do find a teacher who is completely qualified, you are entering into a relationship that is in its very essence hierarchical. You are living with the fundamental assumption, "You have something that I don't have." Even if that were true, there is a way in which that relationship is self-generating. Once the teacher and the student create a dynamic like this together, the roles are set, and it can be very difficult to break them. The teacher may become more and more isolated in an ivory tower of holiness, and the student may embark on a path that just goes around in circles, ever deepening the belief that awakening is out there somewhere: in this other person on a podium, or in a future that never arrives. Satyaa reflects:

> *One of the dangers is that the student can hide behind the teacher, so that being a student becomes another addiction.*

> *I noticed my tendency was to not honor and recognize the light in everyone else as I did in my teacher. I was still in the old paradigm, caught in this cycle of trying to improve myself, always locked into the sense that I have to become better before I am lovable or worthy, or before life can really begin. This is called "seeking." As long as that seeking is going on, there is an experience of lacking something.*

We Are Multi-dimensional Beings

In the last couple of decades, things have changed dramatically. By now, millions of people have had glimpses, at least, of their true nature as limitless. The initial glimpse of spaciousness is not the main focus any more: most of us are much more interested in knowing how to fully participate in day-to-day life from this more expansive consciousness. Satyaa comments:

When I was with teachers in India, the focus was very much on finding that which we truly are. I feel that we are now at a different place historically. People are recognizing with some ease that there is this amazing, spacious, vast, conscious ground of being that we can easily discover, whenever we turn our attention to it. Once we've made that discovery, then the question is "How do we live that in our lives?"

I sense that there is urgency now. We don't have time to waste. The world needs this recognition to spread like wildfire. So my question has become, "How can this be shared in the best, simplest, most direct way with my friends?" I came to participate in Awakening Coaching because I was looking for a container with which I could spread the beauty of this discovery of who we really are. I needed to be able to take into consideration people's longing and talents and where they are in their life; to empower them to live their full potential in their lives.

Today, many people are discovering a fundamentally different way of exploring awakening. We recognize that we are all multi-dimensional beings. Now we have access to the dimension of ourselves that is free and that is one with the source of all life. And, if we are honest, we are also aware of the dimension of ourselves that can still get caught up in the small dramas of life. The problem is not that we have these human characteristics, but that we resist them, we deny them, and we do not tell the truth about them.

Awakening Coaches are not more advanced or more "Enlightened" than others, but simply people who have the humility to step out of the way, and to be present for another human being's evolution and unfolding. This means to be willing to rest in that dimension of themselves that is free, long enough to be of service to another human being. Satyaa says:

> *The Awakening Coach is fully aware that he or she is exactly the same as the other person, except of course for personal details. So there is an intimacy in the relationship, and I think that is what everyone is longing for. It is a true friendship, a true support; it's discovering something new together, rather than thinking someone has been somewhere, and now they've come back to tell us how to climb the mountain.*

> *We are all awakening together from this old trance that has been hovering over humanity. It has been one big misunderstanding, and now we are beautifully empowered by the discovery of this deeper wonderful truth. So let's see how deeply we can be of support to each other. That is what coaching is looking for. We are there with the intention of true support, which means holding a space of acceptance, and pure loving attention.*

The focus is on what is right with you, not on what is broken. The coach meets the client, willing to listen to the story, but also aware of what exists deeper than the story. "I see that there is a temporary drama happening just now that has taken your attention. And I understand that this can be upsetting for you. The same thing happens for me, too. But I know who you really are. I know your true potential. You are limitless, pure, and infinitely creative. Please allow me to remain by your side while this storm is passing, and to remind you of your true home."

Seven Innate Brilliances

Once we understand that anyone can become a support to anyone else for awakening in this way, we see that it has less to do with who is showing up in the meeting, and more to do with how they are showing up.

Over the last twenty years, my friends and colleagues and I have been able to identify seven "Innate Brilliances" that are present whenever anyone is acting as a support and guide to awakening. Anyone can learn how to activate these seven Brilliances easily, and with some practice anyone can become confident and competent in using them. In the next seven short chapters, I will introduce you to each of these qualities in turn, and explain to you how easily you can practice them.

Innate Brilliances

CHAPTER 6

Inspired Certainty

A h, there you are. I see you are looking at that digital photo frame. There are thousands of pictures in there from years back. See that one? That is my younger son and me skiing together, not far from here. I learned to ski when I was already in my 40s, when we moved here to the Sierra Nevada Foothills.

Having grown up in England, I went on a ski slope for the first time in my life at 40 years old,. The second or third time I was there, I booked an individual lesson, and I got assigned to a young man from New Zealand, perhaps 19 or 20 years old.

"G'day, mayt. Moiy naym is Neal. Pleasda meetcha, mate. Folla me to de lift." Before I had time to tell him that the only slope I had been on before was "Bunny Hill," for the small children, we got on the ski lift and went up, and up, and up. After the longest time, it started to level off, and then I realized we were only halfway there. Then we went up, and up, and up, and up some more.

When we got up to the very top of the mountain, we were in a blizzard. In every direction, all I could see was that the terrain was going down, down, down— much steeper than I was comfortable with.

"This is much too difficult for me!" I yelled at him through the blizzard.

"Wotcha say, mate?!" he grinned. "Carn ear yer!"

"TOO DIFFICULT!" I screamed.

"Ah, yule be arite," he yelled back. "Remembah, sverri simple, mayt. Lean onta yah liff lig, and yule go to da liff. Keep ya skis perelil. When ya git as far as ya can to da liff soyd uda slowp, lean to ya roite, and yul go de uda wai." Then he gave me a short demonstration, which looked like ballet.

I tried what he said, and after a few minutes I picked it up. Well, sort of. There was plenty of falling down that day, but I did develop a makeshift way of skiing parallel to the slope, instead of hurtling straight down at breakneck speed to my death.

I made it all the way down the mountain in one trembling piece. It took a long time, and a lot of waiting on Neal's part, but I did reach the bottom alive.

"Dat wernd too bayd for a level-three skeer," he said, when we got back to the lift.

"Level three?" I exclaimed. "I'm barely level one!"

Turned out I had the wrong instructor, and I should never have been up on that mountain in the first place. But even though I was way out of my league and had been put in the wrong class, Neal gave me a valuable gift that day. Sure, he gave me some new tips about skiing. But what was much more important to my survival was that he passed on to me his own sense that it was easy, that anyone could do it. He knew it was easy, and he refused to participate with me in the conversation about how it was too difficult. His confidence was so infectious that simply by naively believing him, believing that I could do it, sure enough it came true for me.

Now, I am sure that you have had moments like that, too. Whether it was a ski instructor, or a teacher at school, or your favorite grandparent, I am sure that at some time someone believed in your potential with such incredible certainty that you became capable of reaching far beyond where your doubts and thoughts would otherwise have kept you. For example, I have written seven books now. This is number eight. But I don't know if I would have written a single book, if I would have had the confidence or the willingness to push through doubt and blocks, were it not for Mr. Coleman, my English teacher when I was thirteen.

Christopher Coleman was a big bear of a man, with a generous overflowing black beard and eyes that twinkled. He used to give us writing assignments for homework, usually short stories about our families or our lives. I remember that when it was time to hand in our homework, Mr. Coleman would take mine and say, "Ah, Ardagh, I always look forward to reading your work." When he would return my assignments to me, handwritten on lined paper, he would write words of encouragement and praise in red ink, followed by his large and completely unreadable signature. Perhaps you can imagine the effect that this kind of attention has on a developing mind? His praise and confidence sent me back after school to exercise my imagination even harder, to focus even more, to do even better.

Christopher Coleman saw something within me, hidden away, and he called it forth. He knew something about my potential and my gifts that I myself was unaware of.

The Sky behind the Clouds

An Awakening Coach brings this same sense of Inspired Certainty, not to your ability to ski or write short stories, or even to your capacity to make money, meet deadlines, or lose weight, but to who you are, deeper than your story. The coach knows that behind the story of "*Me*" and "*My life*" there is an infinite consciousness of pure creativity and potential.

England is famous for being cloudy. There are roughly sixty sunny days a year, and all of the others are overcast, cloudy, hazy, dull, sunless, misty, foggy, dismal, or rainy: all different ways of saying that you cannot see the blue sky or the sun. During the winter in England it can go for weeks and months without a sunny day. It is easy to become depressed. Sunshine and blue skies seem like a far-off dream that you can remember in your mind, but that you can no longer trust were ever real. During those times you might need someone to remind you that the sun is still there and the blue sky is still intact, just obscured by clouds.

Almost anyone is capable of providing such reassurance; it does not take the weatherman. Any good friend has had enough experience to know that clouds are temporary and cannot affect the sky itself. Sure, there are clouds, but we know that the clouds will go away and the blue sky will come back, if we wait a little while.

Strangely enough, the majority of human beings have become so hypnotized by thoughts, fleeting feelings, and unresolved problems which appear to demand immediate solution, that their access to their true nature as limitless consciousness has gone. When the clouds are there, clouds are all there is, and that can be a terrifying and bewildering place to live, with no solutions in sight.

Inspired Certainty simply means that you have had enough of a recognition of the dimension of yourself that is free: the infinity in which finite objects appear, the stillness in which sound is heard, the formlessness in which the body and all other form are created. The recognition is deep enough that it cannot be forgotten. It may not be at the forefront of your attention all the time, but any doubt has evaporated that this is who you really are. The thoughts and feelings are passing in a consciousness that is infinite; the clouds are passing in an infinite blue sky. Once this recognition becomes settled within you about your own thoughts and stories, quite quickly it becomes true about listening to other peoples' thoughts and stories as well.

We need to make an important distinction here, because Inspired Certainty does not mean that you are now somehow permanently in a vacuum, no longer having thoughts or feelings. It simply means that you now know the context in which thoughts and feelings are arising, in yourself and in everybody else. You now know what that means: the little things are dancing in the vastness, and not the other way around.

Inspired Certainty means that a coach, through being in a relationship with another person, can help the other person to restore this context. They intuitively know that freedom is just a breath away. They intuitively know who the client really is, and that knowing guides the other person home.

It is impossible to emphasize enough how important it is to have one or more people always in your life who have this sense of Inspired Certainty.

Beyond the Brain

Now it is time to meet another friend who can tell you about all this from her own personal experience. Karen Fritz has two degrees: one in neuroscience and the other in computer science. She has a very scientific, logical background. She has been academically trained to understand that the physical and measurable world is all that exists; that thoughts and consciousness are created by the physical brain.

One of the most important tools we use in Awakening Coaching is called "Radical Awakening." We will talk about that together very soon, and I will guide you into it myself. When Karen came to train as an Awakening Coach, she had difficulty following the process back to a recognition of the spaciousness beyond thoughts. When she heard the question "Who is experiencing this moment?" she would reply, "my eyes, my ears, my brain." The class practiced Radical Awakening together in pairs for a few hours, so when everyone came back to the meeting room they were all wide-eyed and legless. Karen remembers what happened next:

> *Arjuna, I remember you looked around and said, "Is there anybody who didn't get it?" I raised my hand, and you moved your chair over to face me. You asked me, "Can you hear the sound of my voice?" I said that I could. You asked me, "Who or what is hearing the sound of the voice?"*

I could literally experience it through the ear. "What is experiencing the hearing?" My education popped in with a beautiful diagram of the brain, with every fold and nook and cranny perfectly labeled. I had held a brain in my hand. In my neuroscience training we had human brains that we had to hold. The instructor would point to a particular fold: "This is Wernicke's area. This is where language comes from; this is where language is understood." Every single fold was functional in this very clear model that I had in my head.

So we went around and around and around. You asked me who was experiencing sounds and images, I told you it was my eyes and ears. You asked me who was experiencing the thoughts and images of eyes and ears, I told you it was the brain. You asked me who was experiencing the image of a brain in my mind. As you asked me these questions, I felt I knew all the answers. You kept asking, I kept answering, and we went round and round in a circle.

Finally, you just pulled back. I think you said, "We are going to learn several different portals to awakening; this may not be the best portal for you." And at that point you looked at me and you dropped underneath. It felt like you went into a much bigger space, and because I'd been following you and following you through the dialogue, when you dropped underneath, I just followed you over the edge.

Karen is describing her experience of being invited by a coach into a space, a bigger context, of Inspired Certainty. It is a bit like an Easter egg hunt. When my boys were small, they really wanted to find all the eggs that had been hidden. I knew where they all were, as I had hidden them all, in my alter-ego as the Easter Bunny. I knew very well there was still one more Easter egg, and I knew that it was underneath the urn, behind the mulberry tree, because I had put it there. When they went closer to it, I could say "warmer," and when they went further away, I could say "colder." They might get very frustrated and start to think that there was no last Easter egg, but I absolutely knew that it was there. I could be relaxed about the whole thing, because I knew very well where the last Easter egg was hidden. It really did not matter if they were frustrated or excited: I knew they would get the Easter egg, because I knew where it was.

I had the same certainty sitting with Karen. I could relax in my chair and say to myself, "OK, so this woman has had a strong training in neuroscience. She has been trained to look at the brain a certain way. She knows the names of all the folds. But I absolutely know, beyond any shadow of a doubt, who she really is: she is limitless consciousness. She may or may not agree with that today, she may or may not experience that directly today, but there is no hurry, because I know that is who she is. She will fall into this sooner or later no matter what."

Karen continues:

> On that day I had the tiniest glimpse of freedom, of infinity. It was probably less than a second. I didn't get to rest in it for long before the mind closed back up, but it was a chink in the armor. Over the next six months I used the practices I learned from the training several times a day, which allowed me to build on that experience. In that tiniest of glimpses I knew it was real, I knew I had touched the infinite, but I couldn't return on my own. I had to build the muscle.

One of the reasons that Karen came to the training was because she had battled with depression for many years. She remembers:

> It first hit after I had my second child. It was postpartum depression. And then it was four or five years until I started to get a handle on it through tasting awakening in this way. The last time it hit, I didn't know if it was serotonin not being created, or the onset of menopause, or another story. Who knows what the underlying cause is? Sometimes

it's just chemistry. It's not about beliefs and being all caught up in the mind; it's just chemistry that gets you cloudy. A lot of time it shows up in my body. The tips of my shoulders come forward, and roll in about a centimeter. Then an emotion comes, and I feel sadness or I feel grief. That emotion is clearly coming from chemistry. Then thoughts come in and try to explain the emotion. Now I know, as soon as my shoulders start to roll in, not to believe a damn thing I think.

Depression can be a horrible and debilitating experience. The Inspired Certainty that has grown for Karen allows her to experience these thoughts and emotions as floating in a bigger ocean of awareness. When they come to visit, they can really grab her: it is in her genes. But this recognition of being essentially free has never been eradicated. She could have opted to use this moment of awakening as an escape, but she also recognized that this would have been avoiding that which makes her human. She has chosen to stay open in these states of depression.

Karen now offers Awakening Coaching to small-business owners, both individually and in groups. Though she was once dominated by doubt and concepts herself, Karen has been able to pass on a sense of Inspired Certainty to others. She has a great story:

I remember a young man I met when I was doing a workshop on business planning. I was incorporating all the tools of Awakening Coaching into a workshop on marketing and business development. This man was gay, he was broke, he was a gifted artist, but he was working at a coffee shop as a barista and he hated it. He felt that his boss was abusive. We got into this workshop and I asked some question about money. Some anger came up for him.

"Great!" I said. "Are you willing to address that here in this business planning workshop?"

"Sure," he said. I asked him to come up and sit in a chair across from me. I asked him some of the questions we use in Awakening Coaching. I was holding the space of Inspired Certainty. I knew for sure that he was not the anger. It needed to come up for him, to be expressed. I just sat with him, accepting all that was there for him in the moment. Then I looked at him and I said, "I see you."

He burst into tears.

His whole shell shattered. That was all he needed: to be completely seen, in that moment. All of him. To be completely embraced on that level. In his past, being gay, he had been rejected by his father, he had never been good enough; everything he had done had been wrong. He hadn't been able to be financially successful; he had felt judged by so many people for so many things. To have just one complete moment of being entirely seen, of not being judged: that statement, "I see you," unwound everything that he judged about himself. It made it OK for him to be him. Just as had happened for me in my training, I saw him for who he really was, beyond the story he was telling himself. That is the power of Inspired Certainty.

Asking Powerful Questions

We generally bring the spirit of Inspired Certainty to a coaching session not through lecturing and righteousness, but through holding a presence of relaxed confidence, and through asking powerful questions.

The most immediate example of this would be the question, "Who is experiencing this?" It is an expression of curiosity, not a teaching of a philosophical position. Here is how it might work in practice:

"I really don't know what I want, I feel lost and confused. I don't even know if it's going to work. I don't get the sense we're getting anywhere."

"Good. So this sense of confusion and lostness, this doubt about where we are going, do you feel it in your body?"

"What you mean, in my body?"

"Just scan your body with your awareness, and as you allow yourself to feel lost and confused, notice what is here...."

"There is a sinking feeling in my chest. It feels heavy and empty."

"Good. Now tell me, are you aware of this sinking feeling in your chest?"

"What do you mean? Yes, the feeling is definitely there."

"Good. So say the words 'I can feel a sinking feeling in my chest.'"

"I can feel a sinking feeling in my chest."

"Good. So now just allow the attention to shift from the sinking feeling to that which is feeling it. What is aware of the sinking feeling?"

(a pause)

"Something like a lost child."

"OK, now in this moment, this lost child, does it seem to be more like a thought, an image, or a body sensation?"

"Yes, I can see a sad child, kind of bunched up and afraid."

"Are you aware of this image of the lost child?"

"Yes."

"So simply shift the attention from the image of the lost child to that which is aware. Who is noticing this image?"

"I am."

"Great. 'I am.' So now take the attention and direct it to this 'I.' What is it? How big is it? What color is it? What texture does it have?"

"I don't know. It feels very still now. It feels very expanded."

There are literally hundreds of questions that a coach can bring to a client to guide them gently from being caught in the trance of thoughts and beliefs to the open skies of spacious consciousness. It really does not matter where we start. Whatever it is, it is being experienced. Powerful questions asked from Inspired Certainty move the attention from things that shift and change to the consciousness that is still.

So, this is Inspired Certainty. You know what is possible. You see so clearly the hidden brilliance in another person that just the seeing of it brings it forth. This is the first and most important quality of Awakening Coaching. You see behind the story of "Me" and "My life" into infinite consciousness and potential. You know absolutely that your client is the sky, coming to see you in your office, dressed up as a cloud. You are willing to participate in the cloud conversation, but you know without a doubt that the sky is also here. This absolute certainty about who you are, and who the client is, becomes infectious and the foundation for awakening consciousness.

CHAPTER 7

Absolute Presence

The second Innate Brilliance which anyone can easily learn, to become a facilitator of awakening for anyone else, we call Absolute Presence. It means to hold a space of presence for another person that is so strong, so unshakeable, that it becomes infectious. The presence becomes stronger than the story.

The best way to get a feeling of how powerful this can be, for you or for anyone, is to allow me to introduce you to another amazing person. You see that woman sitting over there, listening to the man talking to her? See how she is leaning forward just a little bit toward him; how her gaze is softly with him, not looking away? Her name is Connie Kishbaugh. She has discovered the art of listening with all of herself.

Moving beyond Distraction

I am sure that you have had the experience of talking to someone who is distracted by external things. Have you ever tried to keep up a conversation with someone who at the same time is texting, or cruising Facebook? They may make the required grunt or "aha" now and then, but still, it is frustrating. It feels like you are getting only the tiniest trickle of their attention. We can call this "external distraction."

But even after the cell phone has been put aside, and the laptop has been closed, there is still another kind of distraction, and it can be just as frustrating. You may have experienced it happening within yourself, or you may have met it in another person. That person may be looking right at you, seemingly giving you their attention, but still you can feel that they are not really present. There are all kinds of internal distractions that keep us from being fully present with another person: such as rehearsing what you want to say next, evaluating what the other person is saying, coming up with an argument, or just thinking about something else.

Absolute Presence means that we know how to become free of both external and internal distraction, at least for a while. You may not do this all the time, but when you want to, when you need to, you know how to show up with 100% of you for another person. This is one essential quality of a great Awakening Coach.

The World's Most Stressful Job

I first met Connie in the late 90s, when she was the Senior Research Nurse at UC Davis Medical Center. She had been in that same position for about twelve years. I think her job at that time was one of the most difficult and stressful I can possibly imagine. She worked as a liaison for cancer patients, once all the standard treatments were no longer working. She would accompany them through the process of using new and experimental drugs, although the chances of the patient surviving were less than 3%. Once these experimental drugs also no longer worked, she would help transition her patients over to a hospice program, where they would be allowed to die.

The patients who are put on these kinds of clinical trials are still in what would normally be the middle of their lives. They often have young children, marriages, careers that have only been partially realized. It does not seem like a good time to die just yet. It is very hard for doctors to tell such patients, "There is nothing more that we can do for you," when there is still so much for them to live for. So these patients get put on experimental drugs, and 97% percent of them die in the process anyway. Connie's job was to be an advocate for these patients within the hospital system. Connie tells us how it was for her, before she became a coach:

> *There was a great deal of communication that got missed. The patients didn't want to hear what was being said. And they would often complain*

to me, and not to their physician, about their symptoms. Then the physician would visit them and ask, "How is everything?" and they would reply, "Oh just fine, doc, I'm doing great." So most of the time when I would meet later with the doctor, we each had quite a different picture of how the patient was doing. I would say, "I think we need to start him on something for his appetite." And the doctor would say, "Why? He told me he was eating fine."

It was very stressful, because everyone felt I was not doing my job properly. The doctors felt I was overstepping my boundaries, and making stuff up. The patients felt I was not advocating strongly enough for them. I felt very alone. I took it all very personally, and I had no tools to help me. At the end of the day I would go home feeling I had failed everyone. I was on call 24 hours a day. I had a beeper, and it was with me all the time.

It was in this state of stress and burn-out that Connie came to take the Awakening Coaching Training in 1999. We did not offer it online then; it was a one-week residential course in California. In that week Connie learned the simple art of Absolute Presence. We use a very simple method that has its roots in Tibet, from the *Bön* tradition that even precedes Tibetan Buddhism. The original method is called *tonglen*, and was included in a classic 11th-century text by Atisha. We have adapted it to be suitable for a modern coaching context and we call it "The Heart Meditation." Rather than simply listening or seeing as a passive experience, we teach our coaches how to allow all experience to ride on the breath. On the in-breath, everything is absorbed home, through the window of the heart, into natural presence, into limitless consciousness. On the out-breath, a wave of blessing emanates out of this natural presence into the world of sounds and shapes and movement and feeling.

We always start this practice with ourselves. You begin by absorbing your own thoughts, feelings, and body sensations home into vast presence. Imagine the center of your chest (the "Heart Center") to be something like a window, with thoughts and feelings and all that has shape and form and limits outside the window, and natural vast presence inside the window. Everything gets absorbed in through the window on the in-breath back into formlessness, and everything gets blessed and reborn on the out-breath. As soon as this process starts to flow naturally with your own thoughts and feelings, it is an easy next step to expand the absorbing and blessing to the thoughts and feelings and speech and actions of others.

This method is extremely simple, and can be easily learned by anyone very quickly. The result is that both external and internal distractions evaporate effortlessly, and Absolute Presence remains. If you would like to try it out for yourself, I think it would be better for you to hear the instructions rather than read them. Here is a link to an audio recording[5] I made back in 1995, when I was just a young man with a dream.

The Power of Presence

The week after her training in Awakening Coaching, when Connie went back to her work as a nurse, everything was different:

> If I entered the Heart Meditation very intentionally before I went into the clinic room with the patients, I heard what they were saying to me on a different level. Maybe they were talking about their symptoms, but what they were asking was, "Nurse, am I getting worse? Am I going to die?" Now I could hear their unspoken communication. If they came at me with anger, instead of immediately trying to defend against it, I could just absorb it, not into myself, but into the vast presence. It would break them open. It allowed us to quickly get to what the anger was all about. I wasn't

---

[5] http://better-than-sex.kajabi.com/posts/the-heart-meditation--5

taking it into myself anymore. That was the big difference. Rather than Connie showing up, I had become a vehicle for space. Presence was doing the work now. A weight was lifted; my job was simply to hold presence.

But that was not all. Things changed between the patients and their doctors as well. When I was in the room and holding that space, the communication between the patient and the physician became more real. Nothing changed outwardly in my behavior; I wasn't trying to guide the conversation or speak for the patient. The patient and physician spoke for themselves, but now the patient was able to communicate what his or her needs were, and the physician was able to hear that. That presence was having an impact, in that they were both behaving differently, and they probably didn't know why.

We often think that this kind of dynamic presence is a matter of luck, or a gift of divine grace. Here is the good news: it can be learned; it can become a resource to you that is available when you need it. I have taught this method of coming into Absolute Presence to literally thousands of people. Many of them have used it to become excellent coaches, and many have also used it in other contexts as well.

We generally put so much attention on what we are saying or doing, and on what the other person is saying or doing, that we overlook what everyone is craving for: presence.

Parents try the Heart Meditation with their children and discover that when a child is whining for an ice cream or for a toy or to be picked up, it is really the unwavering presence of the parent, eye-to-eye and heart-to-heart, that will satisfy their craving, and nothing else.

Doctors and psychiatrists and nurses tell me that when they bring the Heart Meditation to their patients, they get to the core of the real cause of all disease: the dis- ease caused simply by people not showing up to where they already are.

When physicians become present to patients, it is an invitation for the patients to become present to themselves.

I remember a business man who regularly had meetings with the sales representatives for his products in other countries. After he learned the power of presence, the reps would schedule the meetings more frequently. Then they started to come from abroad to see him as a whole team for a few days. His orders went up of course, but he knew that nothing had changed with his manufacturing. The reps were so attracted by the space of presence, they kept finding excuses to visit again and again and again, and each time they felt obligated to place another order.

Dying with Grace

But the best story of how powerful Absolute Presence can be comes again from Connie. At the time she took the Awakening Coaching Training, she had a patient named Jeff with lung cancer. He was 42, with a wife and two teenage children. He was a very aggressive lawyer, a partner in his law firm. A "we're-going-to-do-this-my-way" kind of a guy. Let's let Connie tell you what happened:

> When I first met him, Jeff wanted to do everything his way. Every time I went to visit him, in his home in a gated community, we would have a conversation about his smoking. He had lung cancer, he was still smoking, and he wanted to get better. He was insisting that he would get better. His wife felt that if he stopped smoking right now, his cancer would be cured. In reality it wouldn't have made a difference to the cancer; it was already there. It would probably have eased some of his symptoms. All the other treatments had already failed. Whenever we talked about smoking, he became defensive. Then anything I suggested in any other area, like ways to increase his protein intake so he felt more energy or tolerated the chemo better, he would say "no" to as well. He would say "no" to anything I suggested because he was already defensive about the smoking.

It was very difficult for all of us to work with him. Then I did the training. Once I had this tool, the Heart Meditation, every time before I went into the house to be with him I would spend time in the car, consciously deepening into presence. Within a few days, I found that I could suggest things that I had suggested in the past, the same things, but in a different space, and I could just see him relaxing into being able to hear that this could help him.

Then he developed pulmonary embolism: blood clots in the lungs. When I went to see him at home one day, I saw he had these symptoms, so I called the physician and we got him admitted to the hospital right away. I drove behind the ambulance, and arrived soon after they did. I could hear him when I walked onto the hospital floor: he was yelling at the nurse. So I dropped into the Heart Meditation and went into the room. He looked at me and just held out his arms for me.

Connie stops speaking now, and holds back her tears.

I just held him, and he let them do whatever they had to do for him. We sat and we talked. What could this mean about his process? Did it mean he would have to stop the treatment? I told him it was up to him and his physician, it wasn't my decision, and that it could be talked about later.

He recovered quite well. The next time I went to see him at his home, we were able to talk about things we had never been able to before. What would happen to his children? What would he need to do to make things complete with his son and daughter? What would he need to do to make things complete with his wife?

He and his son had the kind of relationship where the son tried, and tried, and tried to please his dad, but nothing pleased Dad because his son wasn't him. His son was a sweet, gentle kind of kid who wanted to be in a band. Jeff saw that as we sat together, and he recognized the expectations he would have to drop in order for his son to feel truly loved and accepted.

His wife was very concerned about their finances. Would she have to give up her home in the gated community, which they didn't own outright? Things like that. He told me that he felt like a failure, leaving them in a place that was not fully secure. He hadn't been able to talk to her about that before: how it made him feel like a failure at being a provider. In his mind up to this point, he was not going to die. He was going to beat this. As far as he was concerned, his wife was just nagging him; he was not going to die and she would be taken care of. Finally, he was able to say to her, "I really feel like I failed, because I haven't provided for you as much I would have liked to." He talked to her, and then he made a deal with one of his other partners. He sold his share in the law firm, so that she would have money. They found a resolution.

In those last days our meetings were very gentle. I would just practice the Heart Meditation, and then I would sit with him. We didn't even have to speak sometimes.

He thanked me every single visit. He said, "Thank you for being here," every time we met. He apologized for how he had been before: "I'm sorry I was so hard on you in the beginning." I never told him I had done this training, or anything about the Heart Meditation. It never seemed appropriate.

This is how Absolute Presence has worked for me with every patient since then, in the last twelve years. It is something for me; I do it internally all the time I am working with someone. It gives patients the space to be themselves, to feel themselves, to forgive themselves, and to make everything right with their world and their people.

Today Connie has retired from her job at the hospital. She works with cancer patients privately, coaching them in their awakening and supporting them either in their recovery or in dying consciously. Now she lives in rural Pennsylvania, but she mostly works with people over the phone and by Skype. Connie supports people now who want to die magnificently and gracefully: letting go, like a dewdrop into the ocean.

CHAPTER 8

Radical Awakening

The third quality that allows anyone to become a powerful lightning rod of awakening for anyone else we call Radical Awakening. It is the capacity to interact with another human being in such a way that they quickly shift from preoccupation with thoughts and feelings, to resting in more expansive awareness — their natural state — in a few minutes.

There are many ways to accomplish this. It is possible to influence anyone in the direction of awakening just through being present with them, and resting in awakening yourself. We spoke about that when we talked about Absolute Presence. It can happen just through soft eye gazing, or a touch infused with energy. It can happen through conscious lovemaking, and in countless other ways.

I want to guide you now into the method we use in Awakening Coaching. When we train coaches, we show them how to go through a series of steps, which are absolutely reliable and repeatable. We have found that anyone with an innocent heart and an open mind can learn the steps and duplicate them with anyone else.

I would love for you to experience this for yourself. There is a page for you, in the readers' website,[6] where you can experience me guiding you through this on video. There is also an audio recording[7] that you can download and play on your MP3 player.

---

[6] http://better-than-sex.kajabi.com/posts/radical-awakening-video
[7] http://better-than-sex.kajabi.com/posts/radical-awakening-audio

Radical Awakening is an extremely simple way to become more aware of what is already here in this moment. Awakening is not a matter of change or improvement: it literally means to become aware of what we were unaware of previously. And that is how we will explore this now.

Let's Dive in Together

In this moment, you are holding a book or an e-reader in your hand. You can see squiggly hieroglyphics on a white page. Is that true? If you look up for a moment, I am sure you can see other things as well: shapes, colors, textures, and movement. If I look up from the desk in my house I can see trees, and the sunlight moving through the trees. What can you see from where you are?

Now I am going to ask you a series of questions. As you hear or read each question, please pause for a moment, long enough to find out what is the honest and accurate answer for you.

The first question: **do you need to think** in order to see an object that is in front of you? For example, hold up your hand in front of your face. Look at the hand. Now that the hand is here, to see the hand, just to see it, not to understand or compare or give it meaning, does it require any thinking on your part?

Now look at something else. Look at this asterisk here, for example:

Unlike words, the asterisk has no meaning. It is just a shape. To see it, just to see it, **is thinking required**? Or is it possible to fully see the shape before you without the need for thought?

Is it possible that seeing in fact occurs without thinking?

In the same way, **does it require any effort, or decision**, to see an object or a shape once it is already in front of you? Take a look at the asterisk again:

Once you have turned the attention to it, does it then require any effort or decision to see what is already here? Take a moment to look around, wherever you are. See the colors. See the movement. See the shapes. Does it require any effort or decision to see what is already in front of you?

Is it possible that seeing also occurs free of decision or effort?

And finally, **is there any time delay**, in your subjective experience, between the object being there and your experience of the object? You need to rely here on your own subjective experience, not what you think or have learned conceptually. When you see the asterisk:

... do you notice any time delay between the asterisk being here and the experience of the asterisk being here? Is it possible that seeing also happens outside of time?

Noticing this about seeing, which is happening now, and now, and now, consider whether it is possible that seeing is actually happening all the time, free of thinking, free of effort, free of decision, free of time.

Could you relax, even now, into being that which is seeing shapes and colors and movement?

Could you relax into being that now?

What is *that*, which we loosely refer to as "me," which is seeing in this moment?

Who, or what, is experiencing this moment?

What Can You Hear?

In the same way, let's investigate together the nature of hearing. When you hear a sound, like a passing car, or a bird outside the window, **do you have to think to hear the sound**? Or would it be true to say that hearing is free of thinking?

As you hear a sound, any sound, **do you have to make an effort** to hear the sound that is already here? Do you say to your body, "OK, start to hear sounds?" Or might it be true that hearing is also effortless, decision-less?

Do you notice any time delay, in your own subjective experience, between the sound and the experience of the sound?

Take a moment to really investigate this for yourself. Hear the sounds now. And notice the process of hearing itself. Does hearing require thought, decision, effort, or time?

Could you relax now into being that which is hearing?

Who is it, or what is it, that is actually experiencing this very moment?

Feel the Sensations in the Body

Finally, we can ask the same questions about the sensations that are happening right now in your body. Take a moment to scan your body. Perhaps you can notice the moisture inside your mouth. Perhaps you can feel sensations of tension or relaxation.

In just the same way, when a sensation is present, **does it require any thought to notice the sensation? Does it require any effort or decision** to be aware of a sensation in the body, once the sensation is already there? **Is there any time delay**, in your subjective experience, between the sensation and the experience of the sensation?

Does feeling require any thought, effort, decision, or time?

Or is feeling also just happening on its own?

Could you relax into being that which is seeing, hearing, and feeling in this very moment, now?

Who is it, or what is it, that is noticing shapes, sounds, and physical sensations in this moment?

Who, or what, is experiencing this moment?

Take some time to investigate this before we continue.

You might like to pause now and go watch the video I have made for you[8], or listen to the audio recording.[9] This may deepen your experience.

Let's Compare Notes

Since 1991, I have asked this same series of questions to tens of thousands of people, not as an intellectual exercise, but as a genuine inquiry to find out what is true, from direct experience. Hopefully, you have had a chance now to find out what is true for you. Let's compare notes on what you discovered for yourself, even if it was only the tiniest taste, and what tens of thousands of other people have discovered as well.

People describe what they discover when they go look for that which is experiencing this moment in various ways. *Consciousness... Spaciousness... Presence... Awareness....*

Like a signpost that has the word "Rome" written on it, these words are pointing to something much bigger than words or concepts. These words are pointing

---

[8] http://better-than-sex.kajabi.com/posts/radical-awakening-video
[9] http://better-than-sex.kajabi.com/posts/radical-awakening-audio

towards a mysterious vastness, empty of content, but full of love and presence. It is this vast presence that is actually experiencing this moment.

For sure, there is also a story here, of a person born in time, and who will also die in time. Both of these exist simultaneously. The important difference is that the story requires thought, whereas the recognition of the presence is free of thought.

Sometimes people say, "I am experiencing this moment. I am. It is me." It is now necessary to investigate this "I" itself. What is it? Does it have any size? Does it have any color? Does it make any sound? Can it be found, from direct experience? Generally, when we investigate in this way, we discover that we have been using the words "I," "me," "mine," and "myself" for our whole lives without really knowing exactly what these words are referring to. When we investigate the "I," when we go look for it, it cannot be found, and the inquiry leads us directly to the spaciousness of consciousness itself.

When people have a glimpse of their "true nature" in this way—as vast, spacious, silent, and completely present—the question often comes up, "How can I keep this in my day-to-day life?" A good coach will help you to discover that this is not the most useful question to ask. A better question would be, "Is it actually possible to make this spaciousness go away in my day-to-day life?" Try it now. Move your hand from left to right. That is a movement, just like all the other movements that you make every day in your life. Did the movement make any difference to the awareness of the movement, to the spaciousness itself?

Go ahead and think any thought you choose. It could be a "positive" thought or a "negative" thought. It doesn't matter. Think any thought you like. Does the thought cause that which is aware of thought to disappear? Does it actually make any difference to the presence itself? Whatever thought arises, there can also be awareness of that thought, and that awareness does not change. That is who you are.

You can conjure up any kind of emotion. Experience the emotion, and then simply notice that you are also aware of the emotion. The emotion makes no difference to the presence.

It is a great practice to spend the rest of your life seeing if there is anything you can experience, think, or feel that could actually make any difference to this vast silent presence itself. You can try bungee jumping, skydiving, or running with the bulls. Wherever you are, there is also awareness of what is happening. The awareness does not change.

An Epidemic of Awakening

Two thousand five hundred years ago, there was a prince in India, named Siddhartha. He was destined to be the next king. But he had such a strong longing that he left everything. He left his wife, his young baby, and his kingdom. He went traveling. He tried everything to find freedom, to find himself.

Finally, he sat down under a bodhi tree one day and he said, "Enough. Enough of this. I'm going to sit down under this tree and I'm not going to stand up until this thing is clear. I'm so done with seeking."

So he sat down. There were thoughts, and thoughts, and thoughts. A thought came of becoming the king. He said to himself, "Oh, that's just my mind." Another thought came of having incredible sex. "It's just my mind," he said to himself again. Another thought came, and another. Finally, in the morning, as the sun was coming up, a sun also arose within him, and he realized one simple thing: "I am not who I thought I was. This prince is here, yes, but that is not who I am. In this moment, it is just a story made of thoughts. I am the awareness that is noticing all of this."

He did not speak English, he spoke Pali. The word in Pali for awareness is *budh*. So he decided, "From this moment on, I am not Siddhartha, I am *Budh*, I am Buddha."

Here is the important point about this story (highly condensed here into four paragraphs): the essence of Buddha's awakening was simply to recognize that his true nature was awareness — nothing more and nothing less than that. Now, it makes an enormous difference how much importance and value are placed upon what is seen in such a moment of awakening. Does it become another temporary experience, another peak moment, another high? Or does it become the very foundation upon which everything else is experienced?

Today millions and millions of people all over the world are having moments of awakening, the essence of which is not different from what Buddha realized under the bodhi tree. I have interviewed hundreds of people whose lives have been irreversibly impacted by such a moment of awakening, and I have surveyed tens of thousands of others. You might have read some of the conclusions I have come to from this research in my other books, especially *The Translucent Revolution*.

Listen now to a few people talking about their experience of the question, "Who is experiencing this?"

Gay Hendricks, a relationship expert, says, "I'm aware of the big emptiness. It is a feeling of space that does not have anything attached to it. I don't really experience a separate person being aware of that."

Sonia Choquette, an expert on intuition, says, "I experience pure energy, a dynamic, breathing, expanding, infinite life energy, that is pregnant with possibility. Everything else dissolves, and any awareness of my personal story no longer exists."

Jack Canfield, an expert on worldly success, says, "I'm simply a pure center of awareness and consciousness. When I pay attention to this which is aware, I experience absolute peace, and presence. I experience myself as expanded as light with no density."

John Gray, the author of *Men are from Mars, Women are from Venus*, says, "When I try to find the me, there is no me. What is there is space. It's a huge space. It's very peaceful, it's very relaxed. It's an infinite, unbounded ocean."

Marci Shimoff, an expert on happiness, says, "There is no definition for who is experiencing this moment. There is energy, there is knowingness, and there is presence, for which there is no definition. It is expansive and silent. It is whole and complete."

These people are not known primarily as spiritual teachers or mystics. You may have heard their names because they are experts in their fields. You can watch a video of many other such people talking about their realization of their true nature here.[10] All over the world, in every walk of life, people are opening to this recognition of their true nature as infinite. For almost all of them, this awakening has happened in the last two decades, since the early 1990s. The challenge now for most of us is not in having peak experiences of awakening, but with making this the most important priority and value, the very foundation of every part of our lives.

Meet Lloyd

Let's go back to the party now. I want to introduce you to another Awakening Coach, who can tell you a little bit about his experience of Radical Awakening. Here is Lloyd Minthorne:

> *Ever since I was little, I have had a lot of deep questions. "Why are we here?" "What are we doing?" "Where does it all come from?" And "Who am I really?" I looked for answers, but I didn't find any that were really satisfying to me. I read a lot of books. I experimented with psychedelics. I met many teachers.*

---

[10] http://better-than-sex.kajabi.com/posts/who-am-i-video

About 15 years ago, I was working as a massage therapist in a chiropractic office. After some months, I discovered that the chiropractor was ripping me off, and I was really upset about this.

One morning I woke up at about four in the morning. I didn't even get dressed. I walked up the hill near my house, still in my pajamas. There were some wild turkeys there, and previously when I would walk there they would run away, but this time they just surrounded me. We walked together to the top of the hill. Sitting there, I had an amazing experience that is really hard to describe in words. I felt like I was filled with incredible love. When I thought of the chiropractor who had cheated me, I felt complete forgiveness. I discovered I am everything, and I am nothing. I realized that this other man was a part of me, so all blame just melted away. I felt filled with love and with energy, and I haven't been the same since. Since then I don't require as much sleep, my diet has changed, as well as many other parts of my life. But later that feeling also started to fade away.

I met Lloyd when I was interviewing people for a course I was creating called Living Awakening. I was interviewing some of the people I just mentioned, about their experience of awakening and how it has become the foundation of their gift to the world. Lloyd still had a massage practice, but he was now also a videographer, and he traveled with me recording these interviews. He remembers that when he heard these people speak about their experience in the interviews, it was similar to what happened to him. It gave him inspiration that he could get back to that same space he discovered on the hill with the turkeys.

I decided to take the Awakening Coaching Training thinking that it could make this opening more predictable, instead of something that came and went. I was blown away fairly quickly. We did an exercise where you look another person in the eye and ask the question, "Who is experiencing this moment?" This inquiry brought me right back into my natural state, in a very effortless, easy way. And now it was easy to reproduce. This was incredibly inspiring to me. My peripheral vision expanded and became clearer. I could tune in to other people more easily. Colors became brighter. I had more energy. Looking into the eyes of another student in the training, I realized that the eyes looking back at me were my own consciousness, looking back at itself.

Everyone had an opening in the training. The majority had very profound experiences of awakening; for a few it was little milder. There was one man who was a police officer. On the first day I asked myself, "What's this guy doing here?" I had some judgments about the police. But the policeman had an awakening just like everybody else. It didn't seem to make any difference what someone's belief system or background was.

I have shared this simple process now with many people. I remember I had a coaching client who wanted to die. She had a lot of health problems, and she wanted to give up. But as soon as I guided her into the recognition of her true nature as limitless, she rediscovered her passion. She wanted to sing, so she formed a band, and now she's the lead vocalist. She still has the health condition, but since we did this Radical Awakening process together, her outlook on life has changed. She came to recognize that there is a dimension of herself that is always here, no matter what's happening with her body. She recognized that her body is like a piece of clothing she is wearing, and not who she really is. It's a paradox: she doesn't want to die now, but she's also more okay with dying than ever before.

Now I introduce all of my massage clients to Radical Awakening. When I give a massage, I ask, "As you are lying on the table, you're experiencing my touch: who is experiencing that touch?" Sometimes this becomes a deep healing experience for them.

Watering the Root

Many people use Radical Awakening in this way: they integrate Awakening Coaching tools into other work they do. It is a little bit like having a plant in your house. You notice that it is looking a little droopy, so you think to yourself, "These leaves looked much shinier and fresher a few days ago." You try to polish the leaves. But it doesn't make a lasting difference. You notice the petals of the flowers are looking a little limp, so you try to freshen them up with some paint. But that doesn't work. You notice that the plant which once had a healthy robust stem is now leaning over a little bit, so you try to brace it up.

You and I both know that the way to take care of a plant is not to worry about the leaves, or the flowers, or the stem. The best way is to pour water on the roots and give the plant sunshine. If you water the roots, the leaves will become shiny and healthy, the flowers will bloom, and the whole plant will thrive.

That is obvious with plants, but it is not always so obvious with human beings. When our relationships start to become full of conflict, we learn to say and do different things, or negotiate different arrangements, with the people we live with. We feel stressed, so we go running or go to the gym. We try all of these different external things. But in just the same way, when any human being is cut off from the source of their own energy, when any human being is cut off from awareness of their own nature, every aspect of their life starts to wither. Their leaves become faded and dull, and their flowers require paint and make-up in order to look good.

Some of the most physically beautiful people I have met in my life were not necessarily young or sexy, and they probably were not wearing any make-up. They were radiating beauty from within. They had an inner radiance, born of connection with their own well-being.

If you work with people, or if you impact people in any way, you can try and listen to them, and solve their problems through understanding, and through advising them on how to change their behavior. But if you know how to help somebody, in a few minutes, to drop deeper than thoughts and feelings, into that infinite reservoir of well-being, you find a way to provide nourishment at the roots, and the rest of their life is nurtured from within.

Some of our great examples of living this awakening come from very different times and cultures. If you live in a cave, with few possessions and no intimate relationships or family, then one moment of Radical Awakening could be enough. You discover your true nature as limitless, and rest as that. But the people we work with in Awakening Coaching have jobs, intimate relationships, kids, parents, money issues, and stress. They also want to participate in the world and make a difference. So the question comes up, again and again, how can I live every aspect of my life enthusiastically from this expansive awareness?

We have discovered, through years of experimentation, that there is really only one thing that gets in the way. I want to tell you now what that is, and the most effective way to deal with it. And I am going to introduce you to another dear friend who can tell you how she has integrated this into her life.

CHAPTER 9

Radical Releasing

Whenever anyone has a moment of true awakening, where awareness genuinely touches into itself, and recognizes itself as infinite and always at peace, it seems to be the end of everything. It is the end of seeking, the end of self-improvement. When you realize, "I am not the person I thought I was, I am actually this vast space," it becomes clear to the heart, and sounds logical to the mind, that there is nothing to do from here on.

This realization would be more than enough if you were going to spend the rest of your life sitting in a cave with your eyes closed. Just sit. In fact, these are the role models we have inherited from other cultures. Someone has a profound awakening, and then they sit in that awakening and become like a statue. Relationships, sexuality, money, social and political action—all drop away. When you look at someone like that, from India, or Tibet, or China, you may see that the awakened one is sitting doing nothing, completely detached, and then feel that there is something wrong with you, something incomplete about your realization, if it is not the same way.

But most of us do not live in caves. We have partners, we have children, we have parents and family, we have work, we have things we feel inspired to create, and that is where life gets a little troublesome. You can ask, with your eyes serenely closed, "Who is experiencing all of this?" There is nothing here. Then you tentatively open one eye, and there they all are: your spouse, your teenage children, your boss, and your clients, all waiting for you to do your stuff.

For many of us, there is a natural disposition towards creating, towards involvement, towards participation, towards making a difference. Sure, sitting quietly doing nothing is just fine now and then for an hour or two, or even for a weekend. But as a lifestyle? Nah.

It is when you are called upon to participate in relationships, in sexuality, in making money, that you are faced with the habits that have defined you as separate. Those habits, when unmet, not only become a cause of suffering, disconnection, and conflict, they also become a way of getting entangled, and we lose contact with being spacious and peaceful. These habits are what we might call "inner obstacles."

Inner obstacles remain largely latent when you are on retreat, or in meditation, or even on vacation. For example, the obstacles that could arise in parenting will not be activated until you have children. Obstacles around dealing with money do not get activated until you have to make financial decisions. Your relationship issues magically evaporate when you live alone. So, in many Oriental cultures, the solution has been to not have children, to not deal with money, to try not to think about sex, and then, hopefully, you won't have to deal with obstacles. For most of us, in the last few decades, this method of trying to graduate from the curriculum by not showing up for class has become unattractive.

If you choose to remain in the game, or if destiny chooses it for you, then you might want to discover what actually gets in the way of remaining as this spacious awareness while engaged in ordinary life. I have investigated this question with thousands of people all over the world.

Some say "thoughts" get in the way. But we have already explored that together. You can, in fact, have any thought you choose, ask yourself who is experiencing it, and quickly discover that thoughts do not cause awareness to go away. The same can be done with emotions. You can evoke great anger and still recognize that it is being experienced by awareness. So what is it? It is not the ego or the mind, because you cannot find anything like that when you really go look. Let's cut to the chase here. Having explored this with so many people, I have found that it always comes back to the same recognition, the same one element that causes the appearance of losing connection with who you really are.

Resistance.

That's it! Whenever a thought, or a feeling, or a situation, or your mother-in-law is met with the idea "This should not be like this," the opposing forces of what is and what should be create a ridge together, a solidity where previously there was a flow, and the appearance of separation is magically created.

Let's not talk too much more about this theoretically. You can find long explanations[11] about how this works in many of my previous books. Let's dive straight into some tools that can begin to dissolve resistance, and to allow us more freedom in living awakening.

Is it True?

The process of melting resistance is really the process of relaxing the grip of our accumulated systems of belief, which we often lump together and call "the mind." We resist things as they are when they conflict with the way we think things should or should not be. The best place to start is to find elegant ways, both alone and with your friends, to question the mind. One way to do this is with the three words "Is it true?"

When you are faced with a limiting belief, the first thing to ask is, "Is this factual, or is it an opinion?" Would everybody agree? An example of a factual statement would be, "Paris is the capital of France." As long as we understand what the words mean, then everybody would say that this is a factually true statement.

"French people are arrogant," on the other hand, is not a factual statement, but an opinion. Not everybody would agree with it, particularly not the French.

---

[11] http://better-than-sex.kajabi.com/posts/the-anatomy-of-belief

This is the first step: are you making a factual statement, or a statement of opinion? Any opinion is an optional belief about reality. Once you see it is an opinion, you can ask yourself a few more questions.

"If I saw this belief on a menu, would I choose it?"

"Would I recommend this belief to a friend, or bequeath it to my children?"

"Have I made any vow to keep this belief?"

"Have I made any agreement with anybody to have allegiance to this belief?"

Keep a little notebook with a small pen in your back pocket. Or use your iPhone. Throughout the day, whenever you notice yourself come up with a belief that not everybody would share, simply write it down in your little book. You might write, "There's not enough time," "Nobody's going to like it," "It's never good enough," "The world is going to the dogs." These are examples of subjective beliefs, which not everybody on the planet would agree with. Simply the recognition that they are opinions and not facts will allow many (but not all) of them to drop away, and you will discover yourself to be right about fewer things, and feeling a whole lot more free.

Could You Let it Go?

A great coach will guide their clients to gradually question and relax the grip of belief. Many points of view will naturally melt away with the question above, "Is it true?" But sometimes there is an emotional charge as well. You are driving on the freeway, running a bit late. You get to a toll booth, and the driver in the car in front of you cannot find any cash. You are stuck, getting more and more impatient. You might blurt out, "What an idiot!" Asking if this is true may not cut it, but there is another question that will.

"Could I let it go? If I had to, if my well-being and that of my family depended upon it, could I just let this position go?" You are not putting yourself under any pressure that you should let it go; you are simply asking, theoretically, could you, if necessary, let it go? Often just considering this question is enough. You find yourself taking a spontaneous deep breath and returning to being spacious again.

There are many bodily practices, such as yoga, receiving massage, dance, running, and swimming, that are physical ways to allow the body the same freedom, to relax a stuck position and to let it go.

Radical Releasing

We have discovered, in Awakening Coaching, that we can release up to eighty percent of the obstacles that appear to inhibit freedom with a combination of these two simple questions, "Is it true?" and "Could you let it go?" But there are some habits of resistance that go so deep in us. No matter how much we ask ourselves questions, the habits persist. So we have developed a simple method, called Radical Releasing, which is highly effective for dissolving stuck positions on things, brings us back to being spacious, and restores freedom of choice.

Radical Releasing is best done with someone to guide you through it and to hold space for you.

So come over here and meet another dear friend. You see that woman over there, standing by the window? Yes, the one laughing, with very twinkly eyes? She was a professional actress for many years in Germany. Her name is Verena Hirschmann. When she first heard about the work that we do, she was completing her master's degree in social work at the University of Mainz. Before coming to Awakening Coaching, she spent years putting off the completion of her studies because she was terrified of the exams. She had tried many methods to deal with this, but nothing worked for her. Here, let's go over and meet her, and let Verena tell you in her own words:

> *I had avoided doing these exams for more than 15 years. I broke up*
> *my studies because I was so scared about exams and couldn't imagine*

going through with them. When I heard about the Awakening Coaching Training, I had all my exams in front of me, and I went to California anyway. I had to go: it was a calling, really. The training was in a very remote area, deep in a redwood forest, surrounded by the biggest trees I had ever seen in my life.

I remember, on the third day, Arjuna demonstrated Radical Releasing with some of the participants. After the demonstrations we divided into small groups to practice with each other. I told my practice partner something about my situation, about my fears, about the upcoming exams. We condensed all these things to one emotionally charged sentence: "I am not good enough." I went deeply into this frequency and felt it. It was in my belly. It was really drawing a strong, painful feeling. The student who was guiding me asked me not just to feel the frequency of it, but to consciously build it up, to make it more. Even though tears came, it was a relief to fully welcome this feeling. After a few minutes I could bring the frequency to the maximum: I couldn't make it any stronger. Then I was asked to just relax, to let go of the thought and feeling and everything, and to return to the question of "Who is experiencing this moment?" I relaxed into being spaciousness. After a minute or two the student asked me to check my belly again, and it was loose and relaxed. I was quite surprised. When I was asked to test the statement "I'm not good enough" again, it was completely neutral, just empty words. We tested the opposite as well, "I'm the best," and that was neutral, too. The whole thing seemed meaningless. When I thought about the exams again, there was no fear.

It turned out to be a lucky move for me that I went to do this training right before my exams. I got home from the training, the exams began, and I was doing Radical Releasing every day on the phone with other students from the training. The thought could still come and go, but it had no charge—it had no hold over me. I went through all the exams, and I graduated.

In those few minutes, I did the exact opposite of what I had always done before. Instead of turning away from the feeling, and trying to control it or to push it away, I drilled down into this feeling, into this frequency, deeper and deeper. I gave this frequency as much space as it wanted. At first this was a little bit scary, but in the end it was an incredible relief. You bring your attention fully to the frequency and make it stronger and stronger and stronger, and then it releases.

I have done a lot of Radical Releases in the meantime—about two hundred and fifty. It has changed my life completely, in every way. It is easier now to connect with other people. There is no need to try and avoid frequencies, because without resistance every frequency is just life, just aliveness. Without resistance there is no suffering from any emotion that is passing. I have become able to do things I never could imagine before: all the things I was longing for, but never dared. I always wanted to talk to people about the things I am passionate about, and I never could imagine speaking in front of people. But I did, and now I do it all the time!

I am a social worker now. I work in Mainz, Germany with immigrant families. I cannot always use these tools in exactly the same way as they are taught in the training, but there have been cases when they have been invaluable.

I was working with a teenager who was having trouble in school. She was generally a good student but she had problems with physics. She was fifteen, came from Nigeria with her parents, two brothers, and a sister. Sometimes the father would hit the children: that was why I was called in. I had to address the violence with the family. Then she asked me privately for help with something at school. She was at risk of failing her physics class. I felt that she was open enough, so I did some Radical Releasing with her. We did it with the sentence, "I hate physics," and we cleared it as well as the opposite, "I love physics." We did the same with "I don't want to learn," and "I love to learn," until they also became equally neutral. Two days later she had an exam in physics and she got a B, where she had been at an F before. She has never had problems with physics again.

I still remember when I asked this young girl from Nigeria, "Who is experiencing this moment?" She answered "Me." I asked her to turn her attention to this "me," and to find out what it is. She relaxed immediately into being spaciousness and silence. It showed me that you don't need to have spiritual beliefs for this to work. You just need an innocent mind and an open heart.

Techniques and Principles

Radical Releasing is a tool for letting go of deeply rooted resistance and relaxing more deeply into the natural state. It works well for most people. It also effectively unblocks barriers to taking action in almost any area of life. It is a tool that is effective because of some basic principles about how you and I and everyone we know are put together.

It is always a good idea to be able to separate the tool from the principle, so that we have freedom to innovate, and do not become overzealous about a particular method. In the same way, Thomas Edison was able to create the light bulb because he understood a fundamental principle about electric power. If we get over-attached to products created by the company he founded (now General Electric), we become dependent consumers. If we can enjoy and integrate the principles he understood and harnessed, we too can become innovators.

I want to share with you some of the basic principles that make Radical Releasing so effective. You can enjoy the benefits of the technique, if you so choose, by contacting one of our practitioners.[12] We could write a whole book about how this works, and in fact I have written several already! So to keep this simple, I will label each principle briefly and then point you to an audio recording where you can hear more.

No. 1. We cling to habits of resistance as if they define us

Once we have defined ourselves, or reality, in a certain way, that definition often becomes more important than the truth. For example, we might have been conditioned to believe "I am a good and honest person." Then defending that definition becomes a lifelong habit. To let go of that position, to tell the truth about thoughts and feelings and even actions that do not conform with "I am a good and honest person," seems tantamount to death. Listen to more here.[13]

No. 2. All beliefs exist as opposites

When we identify with a quality such as "I am rich, I am affluent," we must, inevitability and simultaneously, also create poverty. It is impossible to choose a quality without simultaneously creating the opposite. There is an important difference between trying to change seemingly negative things into positive things and recognizing that they coexist. If we are to be free of one, we must be free of the opposite. Listen to more here.[14]

No. 3. We think that we gather beliefs from experience, but they also create our experience

We assume that things have happened to us, and that as good and objective scientists we have, after painstaking investigation, drawn conclusions about

---

[12] http://awakeningcoachingtraining.com/find-coach

[13] http://better-than-sex.kajabi.com/posts/life-and-death--2

[14] http://better-than-sex.kajabi.com/posts/everything-has-an-opposite--5

reality that stand up to investigation. To be willing to wash ourselves clean of limitation, to return to innocence, it is important to be able to take a step back from our trust in the mind and to consider that it might be the other way around: we come to conclusions first and our experience follows suit. From the points of view we carry, reality mysteriously rearranges itself to prove us right. But if we step back and assume that nothing the mind says is worth relying upon, then we can understand that in fact reality is the manifestation of our thoughts, rather than the thoughts being conclusions drawn from reality. Listen to more here.[15]

No. 4. All points of view can be experienced at four levels at the same time

Any point of view we have about anything at all can be simultaneously experienced at four different levels. Mentally, we experience points of view as beliefs. When we get stuck here, it is very difficult to shift them: they become like attorneys with a stack of evidence to support their fragile position. At the emotional level, we experience points of view as reactive feelings and emotional drama. *You made me feel sad. It's your fault that I am jealous now.* Because feelings are so changeable, it is easier to move out of stuck feelings than out of stuck beliefs. But there is still a story keeping things sticky. Physically, we experience points of view as tension and stuck energy in the body. Anger we sense as a tightness between the shoulder blades, sadness we feel as a pulling inward in the chest, and sexual tension we experience in the lower back.

The fourth way to experience points of view is as pure energetic frequency: a buzzing, an atmosphere, a vibration. Music has such frequency; so do some places. There is no story, just a "vibe." Once we can experience points of view as frequency, they become much easier to release, and that can happen in a few seconds. Listen to more here.[16]

---

[15] http://better-than-sex.kajabi.com/posts/we-create-our-experience--6

[16] http://better-than-sex.kajabi.com/posts/points-of-view-have-levels--9

No. 5. You can feel a frequency without a story

We all know what it is like to feel angry, or sad, or many other emotions. But they are almost always attached to a story: a why and a because. It is rare to experience anger, for example, without a reason for feeling angry. But it is possible, and when we do so we shift to a quantum level where things can appear and disappear for no reason at all.

Back in the 19th century a great Tibetan Lama, Patrul Rimpoche, wrote these words:

> Don't follow after the object of hatred, look at the angry mind.
> Anger, liberated by itself as it arises, is the clear void.
> The clear void is none other than mirror-like wisdom.

Today we can embody and benefit from their meaning in very practical ways. Listen to more here.[17]

No. 6. Whatever you experience fully becomes presence, becomes love

We think we know what anger, or jealousy, or grief are. But really what we are familiar with is the resisted version of these feelings. It is like driving a car with one foot on the accelerator and the other on the brake. A bad smell is always lurking. There is a great and miraculous secret waiting to be discovered here: that anything experienced fully without resistance becomes love itself. Listen to more here.[18]

No. 7. There is no such thing as negative energy

As we experiment with our willingness to experience frequencies without resistance, we discover that the concept of negative and positive was made up by

---

[17] http://better-than-sex.kajabi.com/posts/points-of-view-have-levels--9

[18] http://better-than-sex.kajabi.com/posts/whatever-you-feel-becomes-love--9

moralistic religions and New Age philosophy. When we are willing to welcome and embrace it, everything is, in its essence, a gift and a portal into our own depth. Listen to more here.[19]

No. 8. Pure experience is always now: it has no precedent

Have you ever been sick for a few days, and then someone calls you to ask "How do you feel today," and you answer "Better, thanks." Of course, we speak like this all the time, but here is some interesting news for you—you actually cannot feel "better." You feel as you do, and it is a thought that will follow this feeling, compare it with its memory of yesterday, and decide that one is better than the other. Recognizing this simple fact is a big key to liberating stuck points of view. Listen to more here.[20]

No. 9. Our deepest beliefs are hidden from us

You and I may think we have a pretty good idea about the beliefs that run our lives, but the most powerful and the most limiting ones are completely transparent to us. We are like someone wearing pink-tinted sunglasses, who can no longer recognize the bias in perception, but just sees a pink world and calls it reality. We need support to discover and liberate the core beliefs. Listen to more here.[21]

Try it for Yourself

The best way to experience Radical Releasing is to try it for yourself. In the readers' website you can hear several examples of Radical Releasing[22] happening, and also where you can be guided through the process yourself, as well as find information about how you could contact a practitioner.

---

[19] http://better-than-sex.kajabi.com/posts/there-is-no-such-thing-as-negative-energy

[20] http://better-than-sex.kajabi.com/posts/experience-is-always-now--4

[21] http://better-than-sex.kajabi.com/posts/the-deepest-is-always-hidden--4

[22] http://better-than-sex.kajabi.com/posts/radical-releasing-demonstrations

Here is a summary of the steps we use, which you will hear on the demonstrations:

Step One: Label the point of view or belief as a statement.

"I am weak."
"I am not good enough."

Repeat the statement a few times, until it has charge to it.

Step Two: Where do you feel the charge in the body?
Put your hand on that place in the body.

Step Three: Repeat the statement over and over, and let the charge get stronger.

Step Four: Feel the frequency, the energy, the vibration, the atmosphere.

Step Five: Give it a number from 1 to 10.

Step Six: Keep saying the statement, making the charge stronger.

Step Seven: Continue until it cannot be any stronger.

Step Eight: Relax completely, let the statement go, and ask the question, "Who is experiencing this moment?"

Step Nine: Cut the tape that connects one moment to the next.

If what we are doing here together was like a film or a tape going through a machine, could you, just could you, cut the tape that connects one moment to the next? Could you feel a sensation in this moment without comparing it with another moment?

Step Ten: Bring your hand back to your body. Is there any charge?

Step Eleven: Repeat the statement from Step One.
Does it have any meaning, any charge?

Step Twelve: Check the opposite statement.

"I am strong."
"I am good enough."

Does either one have any meaning or charge?

Step Thirteen: Go back and forth.

Alternate between saying the original statement and its opposite, to see if there is any difference, or fluctuation in energy.

Step Fourteen: Test the stimulus that was creating the resistance.

Now imagine, or remember, the situation or the memory that was associated with the charge, to see if it still creates any reaction.

CHAPTER 10

Empowerment Practices

We have met a lot of people here today. It might be a little overwhelming. Let's go sit down together for a few minutes, and I will tell you about another step in the coaching process.

Remember that we talked about how just one moment of Radical Awakening can seem like the end of the story? How it may seem that now you can just rest as nothing and everything, and only peace remains? Soon you discover, however, there are unconscious points of view that run your life; stories we all try to block out and resist. You come to discover that you are run by "I am not good enough," or "There is not enough time," or "No one loves me," and all the other things you have not wanted to feel and face. You learn to admit that you have been resisting aspects of your experience, and to let that resistance go.

There are literally thousands of these possible fleeting points of view, or "frequencies," that you can resist and then become trapped by. It is very unlikely that you could relax all resistance, once and forever, and be absolutely, permanently, immaculately, once-and-for-all released. First, as you move through life and sing your song and give your gift, you will inevitably sometimes feel frustrated, hurt, rejected, or shocked, and then new frequencies will become sticky and meet resistance. Second, the more of these frequencies you release within yourself, the more your boundaries and defenses relax, and the more you feel a sense of compassion, or oneness, for all of humanity, for all that is alive. In this way, you come to discover that these frequencies are not really "yours"—they are universal. Absolutely everyone has moments of "I am not good enough," "No one loves me," or "It's all too much." You did not choose these frequencies, and you cannot make them disappear. They are all part of a "universal mind" that everyone has access to, but that you do not need to be defined by. In order to live in freedom in every area of life, to love and laugh and give your gifts fully, an additional step is needed.

Let's take the example of "Don't leave me," which many people resist feeling and then become trapped inside. It is quite easy for a well-trained Awakening Coach to help you to build up that frequency to a maximum in a few minutes, and then to relax so deeply that it dissolves, and leaves just empty space. Your coach can also test the opposite of "Leave me alone," with which it almost always co-exists, and dissolve that, too. You are free! Neither one has a charge anymore.

When you get back to your spouse, however, or your children, or your co-workers, you are familiar with interacting with those people in a certain way. You can easily stay caught in limiting patterns of behavior out of habit. Everyone around you is used to these habits, too, so if you tweak them just a little bit, it can throw the whole social environment out of balance.

Some of these habits have been with you since you were a child. Decades of not wanting to ever experience "Don't leave me" will cause you to relate to others from habits of control, or neediness, or being a "pleaser." Many of us have made the mistake of thinking that an inner process that gives us a taste of freedom will suddenly and magically make everything instantly well: now we are free to get on with life, have fantastic relationships, make lots of money, have great sex, and make a big difference to the world. That rarely turns out to be true.

A good coach will bring to you this one fundamental question: If you have been trapped for decades inside resistance to this feeling, and now that resistance is gone, what new freedom does this give you? If you can really welcome this frequency now, as well as its opposite, what can you now do that you could not do before? What can you now say, and think, and feel, that before was impossible? To be able to live every aspect of your life from this new freedom is the reason why your coach will give you Empowerment Practices.

Real-Life Examples

The best way to understand this new freedom is with some real-life examples, from coaching sessions with me and other coaches, of how Radical Releasing naturally flows into specific and tailor-made practices. You can find dozens of examples of these kinds of practices in my book Leap before You Look.[23]

"There is not enough time." Although Larry was retired from his position as a mortgage broker, he still found himself constantly under time pressure, creating tasks on endless "to-do" lists, and so recreating an artificial sense of deadlines. Once he and his coach had dissolved the resistance to the frequency, his coach gave him a practice called "Stop." At randomly created intervals, his cell phone would set off a reminder: after an hour, after another three hours and twelve minutes, and again after another fifty-five minutes. Then he was asked to just stop: to do nothing but breathe and feel and experience sensations in his body for five minutes. Within a couple of weeks he was able to experience how the wheels were spinning within himself, and the sense of pressure diminished.

"They are all idiots." When Michele started to coach with me, she had been through five personal assistants in less than two years. Her unconscious habit was to see everyone around her as incompetent. Because she resisted and condemned her fear of not being able to trust people, it built an emotional charge around it. The more she did not want to be critical and impatient, the more destructive her outbursts would become, the more she hated herself for it, and the more

---

[23] http://better-than-sex.kajabi.com/posts/leap-before-you-look

she traumatized her staff. It did not take much for us to build the frequency of "They are all idiots" to a maximum, and then to take the charge off both ends of the spectrum. The Empowerment Practice we agreed on was to consciously give appreciation. I suggested that she explicitly tell her assistant that she was doing a practice for a while, in which she was to appreciate five things about how she was getting support.

"Don't laugh at me." Pablo came from a large family: he was the youngest of eight boys. His brothers made him the joke of the family, and he hated it. He was a smart boy, and eventually became a university professor. The resistance to looking foolish still ran his life. He created an identity as a very serious and respectable man. This worked out at his job, but with his girlfriend and in his personal life he felt very restricted. We worked with the frequencies of "Don't laugh at me" and "Please laugh at me" until the tension between them was gone, and he could experience either one almost as though they were both someone else's thoughts. The practice I suggested for Pablo needed to be done only once, like taking a high-potency homeopathic medicine.

Pablo regularly gave lectures at the university to hundreds of students. Before the next one, I asked him to go to the costume store and find an animal tail. I asked him to attach this to the back of his pants, so that it extended below his suit jacket. When he started the lecture, he was facing the students. Everything was normal. But when he turned to write something on the white board behind him, his tail was on view to all. There were small whispers, muffled laughter. Cell phones were discreetly brought out. Videos were shot. I asked him to remain in his normal teaching mode and to say nothing about his tail.

This one practice, which lasted for only an hour, changed Pablo's life forever. He quickly lost his reputation for being the stiff and serious professor on the campus. This was the professor who wore a tail. As seen on Facebook. Students and other staff joked with him more often.

When new clients come to me for coaching, I try to explain to them that this work can be very dangerous to their identity: that things may never be the same again. Sometimes I tell them the story of Serious Pablo, and ask them if they would also be willing to die as the old and be reborn as someone new.

"I am too much." Miriam is a woman with strong feelings. When she is angry, it comes like a tsunami, out of nowhere. When she is sad, it feels to her sometimes that she could drown in an ocean of tears. As a child, she was frequently told that her feelings were too much. Miriam learned from her father that she needed to have a good reason for every feeling. As she got older, she felt guilty for, and embarrassed about, her feelings, and developed ways to control them, until they overcame her censorship and burst out anyway.

We dissolved the charge around "I am too much" as well as "I am not enough," so they both became neutral. Now it was time to get into some Empowerment Practices that could give her new freedom to breathe and express herself.

Miriam worked with two practices in the couple of weeks after we dissolved these charges. First, I asked her to write down twelve feelings as different from each other as possible. She came back with *"angry, sad, excited, frustrated, hopeless...."* Next, I asked her to go to her iTunes music library, to choose one piece of music for each of these feelings, and to compile them into a playlist. Twice a week, she switched off the phone and the Internet, locked the door of her apartment, and put on this playlist. She entered into each of these feelings, for a few minutes at a time, for no reason. She learned how to feel—in fact she learned how to create feeling from within herself—without needing to have any reason or story. I invited her to let go of the need to be appropriate.

There was another phase to Miriam's Empowerment Practices. I also suggested that she pay close attention for a little while to the feelings that are always passing within her. For just a few minutes a day, when she was with people, I suggested that she tell the people around her what she was feeling as she noticed it. When she noticed a wave of anger, she would say "Now I feel angry." Whenever she noticed grief, she would tell others about it. If anyone asked her why she was feeling that way, she would say, "There is no reason, I just feel angry right now. I am enjoying it, and it will pass." In this way, Miriam learned to become friendly with her feelings again in quite a short time, and as a result her heart opened, and she was better able to share her true gifts.

À la carte

There are literally as many possible Empowerment Practices as there are coaching clients. This is not a fixed menu: every practice is à la carte. Probably this is the most important skill that an Awakening Coach brings to their clients: with an artful mixture of intuition, compassion, and humor the coach finds just the right practices that will stretch and slightly challenge the client, without sending anyone into stress and resistance.

As you might have already noticed, Empowerment Practices fall into some broad categories. Some are practices to use one time only, to break through a fear of something you have always avoided, and so to experience new possibilities of freedom. Pablo and his tail would be a good example. Other practices may also be one-time events, giving you permission to do something you have always longed for, that has always felt natural, but you have avoided through feeling unworthy, or concepts of what is not allowed. For example, Sarah never allowed herself to sleep in or even to take a day off. She would have loved to, but ran on the idea that "Idleness is the Devil's work." After doing Radical Releasing, her practice was to stay in bed for an entire Sunday, watching soaps on the TV and reading *Oprah* magazine. She needed to do this only once to come out the other side and be free of her censorship of resting.

Other practices do not work in this way: they are more of a drip-feed approach, and most effective when done for a few minutes a day. Years ago, when my wife and I were first together, we noticed that I had a subtle and covert tendency to be possessive. This was British-style jealousy: not in-your-face, but suspicious only in peripheral vision. *"Were you on the phone, dear? Great, great. Who were you talking to … oh, a friend, wonderful. Yes. Anyone I know?... Ah, someone from the past. Good. Good. Well, just tell me, was it a man or a woman…?"* I needed a practice, for a few minutes a day, to fully live out-loud what was otherwise undercover. So we invented Luigi, from Napoli. Every day, for just five minutes, I had the freedom to become over-the-top jealous. In my thick Napoli accent, I would say to her, *"Leeestena, beeetcha. You ara mai wooomana. Okai? You donta lukata eeyni uder man, Okai? Onli meya, onli Luigi. Eh, you chit ona meya, and I keel u, and de uder gai tooa, Okai?"* We had a lot of fun with Luigi, and in a short period of time jealousy ceased to be an issue. It was something to laugh about, rather than to be embarrassed by.

You might also receive practices to live into new and creative habits, just for a few minutes a day. When Michele was asked to give appreciation every day for a few minutes, she was exercising a weak muscle.

Basic Principles

Although every coaching client receives a unique and tailor-made set of Empowerment Practices, there are some universal principles underlying the art of giving these practices. Let's briefly label some of them here.

- **An Acquired Art.** Some of the other skills I have described to you in this book are quite easy to learn in a few weeks. Giving Empowerment Practices is an art form that takes a little more time and practice to become really skilled at. Perhaps you have heard the story about the apartment building in New York. It was a thirty-story brownstone, built in the nineteenth century, with an old heating furnace in the basement. One day the furnace broke down, so the building manager called in a repairman. When he arrived, the repairman spent a few minutes looking all around the basement at the maze of pipes and vents. Finally, he took out a hammer from his bag and hit one pipe in the corner with a sharp blow. The entire system shuddered back into working order. He closed his bag again, and wrote out a bill for $1,000. The building manager objected loudly: "You were only here for five minutes!" The repairman nodded, and ripped up the bill. He wrote out another one: "Fee for on-site visit to hit pipe with hammer: $10. Fee for knowing which pipe to hit: $990." A great coach knows which of your pipes needs a good strong tap to get your whole mechanism of creativity, love, and aliveness working again. Knowing which pipe to hit is an acquired art.

- **Testing Freedom.** The question that underlies these practices is always: What would this person now be able to do if they were truly free of the resistance and restriction within themselves? Because of this, practices are a good way to distinguish between temporary altered peak states, and more stable advanced stages of real evolution and maturity. For example, someone could spend their whole life resisting the sense of "There is something wrong with me," and then be completely run by the unwillingness to feel this frequency. Some people build complex and impenetrable lives to prove to themselves and everyone else that they are really OK. Drinking, sex, fame, money, narcotics—there is an endless menu of ways to prop up the façade and avoid dealing with the unstable foundation. But then the feeling comes back again, and needs endlessly stronger medication. If someone were really and truly free of resisting this feeling, what could they do? They could probably sit for an hour in dirty clothes outside of Safeway begging for loose change and not have it be a problem. They could probably invite honest feedback from people they know they have hurt in the past, one person a day for a couple of weeks, and see it as a positive experience. Practices are a way to test how deep the new freedom is.

- **Forging New Neural Pathways.** Practices do not only test the depth of new-found freedom, they also strengthen weak muscles and allow you to explore parts of yourself that may have atrophied or been dormant for decades. Ironically, some of these weak areas may also be your deepest strengths, which were shut down early in your life. Françoise, for example, was an extremely creative child. She painted at school, made music, did pottery, collage, and sculpture. But like all of us, she was conditioned by her family and culture, and the cold, austere surroundings of Minnesota in the 1960s led to her being ridiculed for her budding creative energy. She struggled her whole life, always trying to find her real gift, and always denying her early love of art. Once we got some opening with Radical Awakening and Radical Releasing, her practice was simply to take an art class, once a week, and to paint for a minimum of fifteen minutes a day. That commitment was enough to lay down new neural pathways, and after six months she had her first exhibition. Once these pathways were opened up, there was little chance that they would close again. Now she exhibits her work regularly and is a full-time artist.

- **One of a Kind.** As we have already discussed, the most important thing about these kinds of practices is that they are all personalized. This makes a coaching approach to living awakening fundamentally different from the old "one-size-fits-all" model, where everyone chants the same mantra, or does the same set of yoga postures, or reads the same texts. One person's nourishment can easily be another person's poison, and the perfect practice for you this week might have been way too difficult and stressful last week, and could become boring and redundant next week. Coaching is a collaborative and personalized process.

- **Mutually Agreeable.** When the practice fits perfectly, it will feel like an obviously good idea to both the coach and the client. A perfect practice will not harm anyone anywhere, but will bring more aliveness, humor, and creative possibility to everyone involved. There is a certain kind of "ding" that happens when you hit the right practice. The person receiving the practice often will laugh out loud, with excitement as well as a sense of "Busted. You got me. You nailed it."

- **Homeopathic.** The right practice is short: a few minutes a day for a couple of weeks, or occasionally a one-time event of an hour or two. It is all a matter of leverage. A small dose of the right practice can be much more effective than trying to become a different person all day long. If the practice is going to work, it will generally do so within two weeks. By that point you have become a subtly different person. I asked Michele to give five appreciations a day for a couple of weeks. And it worked. Combined with her Radical Releasing, her lifelong habit to fear other peoples' incompetence dissolved. If I had asked her to be kind and patient all day long, that would have become too much of a challenge immediately, and she would have hit so much resistance that she would have been left only with a sense of failure and hopelessness.

- **Accountability.** Finally, it is of great importance to have someone to report back to. In Awakening Coaching, the client will have five or six practices to do in a two-week period that might take twenty or thirty minutes a day in total. Each day the client sends their coach a short report. It is just like going to the gym. If you have a trainer to report to, the chances of showing up are dramatically increased. Left in a vacuum, it is easy to postpone and procrastinate, and the sense of being restrained by forces outside of your control gets stronger. By having daily reports, a coach can tweak Empowerment Practices to get them "just right." If they are too challenging, the client will feel overwhelmed and stressed, and will quickly give up. If the practices are too easy, there will be no sense of challenge at all, and the client will get bored and feel that the coaching is not effective. Finding that sweet spot between too challenging and too easy is what makes a great coach.

Meet Katharina

We have been sitting here for a while talking about practices, and look, a whole lot more people have arrived at the party. Let me introduce you to Katharina Rieder, from Vienna, Austria. Katharina loves to give practices in her coaching, in part perhaps because her own experience was so strong:

Hello, pleased to meet you. I live in Vienna, but I flew to Stockholm in Sweden to train as an Awakening Coach. Although I was very interested in and attracted to this way of working with people, I was convinced that I would never make it as a coach. This was a habit for me, of feeling that I would never do anything right, like I was convinced I was a basket case. It was quite unrealistic, as I was well educated in neuroscience. I got to do Radical Releasing on the third day of the training, first with the statement "I'm never going to make it," and then on the opposite, "I am going to make it." I was surprised how easy it was to take the charge off both of these, so neither statement made any sense anymore.

When we all came back from our practice groups, it was lunchtime. I remember Arjuna was suggesting practices to everyone, to demonstrate how practices flow easily from Radical Releasing. Later we also learned to give practices to each other. When it was my turn, he asked the group, "If that charge is completely gone, the terror of 'I'm not going to make it,' what should she now be able to do? What does she now have the freedom to live into?"

There was some discussion about what would be the best thing. Finally, it was decided that for the whole lunch break, which was about two hours, I should act like someone with brain damage. When I first heard this idea, I was shocked. I had no idea what that should look like. It felt politically incorrect, to pretend to be retarded. But at the same time there was a reaction in my body—I burst out laughing. It seemed very funny, and I felt a great relief. Just hearing the idea, something inside me was freed up already.

We walked together, very slowly, the few blocks from the training facility to the restaurant. Almost all of the other students were Swedish, and were talking in Swedish, which made it easier for me to do the practice. It gave me the freedom to forget all about what is correct or appropriate, and to do whatever I wanted in each moment. I did crazy things, like shocking other people in the street, or walking with a completely distorted face, or saying nonsensical words to another person. I was very clear that I didn't care anymore what anyone else was thinking about me.

In the beginning it was a challenge, but with time it became fun. I found the humor in everything. I was observing people in the restaurant and I was imitating them by exaggerating what they were doing. Some people looked irritated, but for the first time in my life I didn't care. I knew it was a practice and I saw the reaction without any emotion. I realized how much I really do care what other people think about me, even people I don't know, whom I will never meet again. It freed up a lot in me.

I was sitting with two other students from the training. One was a lawyer, a very straightforward guy. He had to support me, and he was worried people could react in a strange way. We both ordered a coffee, exactly the same coffee. The waitress came and put them down on the table: one in front of me, and one in front of him. I exchanged the coffees. "His is much better than mine. I want the other one." The waitress tried to explain that they were the same. She was very kind and patient, because she could tell that I had some kind of brain damage. I learned that when you adopt a certain personality, or role, people quickly cooperate with it. When you become a crazy person, the world allows you to be that. It mirrors back to you the identity you project. The funny thing is that we came back to the same restaurant two days later, and I was now acting normally. That confused the waitress no end.

On the way back from the restaurant, I had a lot of fun hiding behind a very big pile of snow. I waited for my friends, and one second before they came, I jumped out and made a crazy noise. I did many things like that, like a little child, the same things that my son does every day. It was very freeing. A lot of creativity was flowing through me. For two hours, every few minutes there was something new.

There was a huge shift in me after this one practice. That pressure of needing to "make it" has evaporated completely since that day. I don't care so much anymore, and things happen more spontaneously. Most of my life I have been a very shy person; it was not easy for me to connect with strangers. That day in Sweden I experienced that it was all coming from my fear of what people would think about me, and once I let go of caring about that, it was a huge relief.

Now I love to give these kinds of crazy practices as a coach. There is an instant release of energy when I give the practice; very often people start to laugh. Just today I did Radical Releasing with a coaching client on "I'm not important" and its opposite, "I am important." At the end I gave her the practice that when her husband is watching football, she should stand up in front of the TV for a few minutes, waving her arms in huge dramatic gestures, giving him no chance to see anything of the game, and sing to him like an opera singer with the words "I am more important and interesting than football."

There are more than a thousand Awakening Coaches all over the world, each giving these kinds of Empowerment Practices to their coaching clients. So the next time you see a man in a business suit playing hopscotch in the street with some children, or a shy woman who suddenly stands up in a crowded restaurant and starts to sing a Britney Spears song, using the pepper grinder as a microphone, they may be completing assignments given to them by their coach.

The more you taste freedom without any boundaries as your natural state of being, the more you recognize and dissolve habits of resistance, and the more you ground this new consciousness in your day-to-day life with practices, the more something new opens within you, like a flower pushing up through cracked earth. You realize that everything we have talked about so far was only a preparation for the main event, for why you are really here. There is a unique gift within you, waiting to be released. As soon as it is activated, your whole world is lit up all at once.

CHAPTER 11

Midwifing the Unique Gift

Everything we have described so far contributes to getting yourself and your life back on track. Once you have easy access to the dimension of yourself that is infinite, once you know how to recognize and dissolve the blocks that get in the way of your true nature expressing itself, once you have tailor-made practices to replace automatic habits with new creative possibilities, it may seem like the job is done. On a scale from one to ten, your life is now a twelve.

And yet.... Yes, there is another "and yet." You can have your money flowing well, be in great health, have good relationships with your family and spouse, and still have a profound sense of something missing in your life. And, although this blows a lot of spiritual theories, you can also have good access to infinite consciousness—a really great capacity to meditate and to disappear like a dewdrop into the ocean—and still feel that something is missing in your life.

As you may know, over the last two decades I have done hundreds of interviews with people who are experiencing extraordinary levels of fulfillment. Nothing is missing. Everything is incredibly wonderful. So what is the key? What is that pivotal thing that makes all the difference between a life that looks good on paper and an overwhelming sense of gratitude, fulfillment, and flow?

The answer does not have much to do with great sex, or money, or fame. It has more to do with the impact you are having on other people. People who have an extraordinary sense of fulfillment, where each day ends with a sense of, "Ah! I've lived fully today," usually can feel and know that they're making a profound impact on others. They are giving a lot. By researching this in interviews for books, as well as noticing it with my own coaching clients and students, I have come to realize that everybody on this planet, with no exceptions, was born to give a unique gift.

Not Always What You Love

There is a philosophy in the world of New Age spirituality that advocates following your bliss. The idea is that if you always do what gives you most pleasure, it will lead to a happy and successful life, and you will earn lots of money, too. "Do what you love," advocated one book in this genre, "the money will follow." My experience of working with thousands of people over the last couple of decades has led me to deeply question this idea. I meet many people who are careful to spend as much time as they possibly can doing things that give them pleasure, and avoiding things that are painful, difficult, or stressful. They go out of their way to protect themselves from what they perceive as negative energy. But the money does not flow easily, nor do these people feel spectacularly fulfilled.

In India, giving the gift you were born to give is often referred to as "following your dharma." In the *Bhagavad Gita*, Krishna advises Arjuna to follow his dharma in the Kurukshetra battle. Arjuna did not want to fight, but it was his duty; it was his role in the bigger order of things. We are faced with moments like this all the time. When your child is in danger, when an important project has been left outside and it starts to rain, or when a team of people are counting on you to meet a deadline, you probably do not ask yourself in that moment what would give you the most immediate pleasure. You do what needs to be done. As a result, you experience something even more important than getting pleasure and avoiding pain: you discover integrity and a sense of purpose.

Remember Connie, who we met a little earlier? She worked at UC Davis Medical Center for decades with terminally ill cancer patients. Looking back on her job now, she remembers that it almost killed her. It was the most stressful job she could possibly imagine. She had a beeper with her 24 hours a day, and if it went off she had to be somewhere quickly. Almost every patient she worked with died. But she made an enormous contribution to those people. She guided so many people, some with young children and lives that seemed shockingly incomplete, to face death in a loving way. She would never say this process was pleasurable. But she knew without a doubt that serving people in this way was what she was supposed to be doing, her destiny, a big part of why she came on this planet. By living her "dharma" her stress diminished, but she was never motivated by self-interest.

Here is the key. The unique gift you were born to bring into the world has a gift label on it. Just like under the Christmas tree, there is a "from" name and a "to" name on the label. Your name is there as the giver, but you are not the recipient of your unique gift. It comes from you, and it benefits all who come close to you.

No One Else Like You

Take a moment and have a look at your right thumb. Now turn it over, so you can see the underneath. You can see lots of squiggly lines there. There are seven billion people on this planet, and none of them have the same thumb print as you do. At a crime scene when police obtain prints, they can match them to just one person. Not only that: my childhood friend who now works at Scotland Yard tells me there has never been anyone in all of history who has had the same prints as you. Among all the humans who have ever lived, you are unique. In just the same way, no one has quite the same face or body as you have. People may look alike, but even with identical twins you can learn to tell the difference.

You also have a unique energetic blueprint. There is a song that only you can sing, a dance that only you can dance. One of the roles of a facilitator of awakening is to recognize that unique gift, through the layers of accumulated rubble and debris from years of conditioning, and to help bring it forth. The tragic thing is that although we all have this unique gift to give, many people live their lives and die without it being passed on.

Before we continue, let's clarify something. When we speak of a unique gift, it could be what you do for a living, but not necessarily. In a minority of cases the unique gift and your source of income are perfectly aligned, but often they are different. Your unique gift is the particular quality, the particular flavor, that you brought to the planet, before you were conditioned in any way.

You may sense the unique gift in a small child of two or three years old, or sometimes even in a newborn baby. Each child has unique characteristics. You probably would not say to the parents, "Oh, what a lovely child. What does your child do for a living?" It is not a relevant question. A child eats and sleeps and plays—lots and lots of playing. The child's unique gift is the special contribution their presence brings to family and friends. Very likely this gift is tied to a particular way of bringing more brightness, more aliveness, more humor, more warmth, and more tenderness into a situation. In the same way, your own unique gift may flow more when you are relaxed and playful. It may flow most abundantly when you are on vacation, or taking it easy at home. You are not working then, you are not doing your job, and the gift may become stronger.

For most of us, the unique gift usually gets covered over by what other people think we should do with our life, by the many sensible and practical fears and concerns about how to survive in a dog-eats-dog economy. And so it is, for most of us, that by the time we become adults, our unique gifts and what we spend our time doing are disconnected.

Hardly a day goes by without my wife Chameli and me giving thanks for our blessings. We have each other, we have two splendid young men we have raised together, we have a lovely home. But most important, we are aware of the privilege we share to spend each moment of each day doing what we are most passionate about. You know that old campfire question, "What would you do with your life if you had a million dollars and you did not need to work?" We would both do exactly what we are doing now. But we do not take this for granted for an instant. We are aware that this is a rare blessing in today's world. This area is the most important that coaching can address.

When I reflect on my own good fortune, I often look back on the lives of my two grandfathers.

Desmond, my mother's father, grew up in Northern Ireland on a big estate. He loved the outdoors; he was fascinated by plants, by the magic of how living things grow out of the earth. This love was his unique gift, a big part of why he was born. In his teens, he had the idea of starting a market garden on his family estate that would allow him to work with plants, fruits, and vegetables, as he loved. But his father did not see that as a suitable profession for someone of his "social class" in Northern Ireland in that time. He was sent to become a stockbroker in London. In 1928, the market crashed, and a couple of years later my grandfather had a nervous breakdown. He never really recovered. Although he still managed to become the secretary of the Flyfishers' Club in London, for his whole life he regretted not having done what he really loved. When he retired, around the time I knew him best, he spent most of his day tending to his garden. Desmond never got to live his dream, to make the contribution he wanted to.

My grandfather on my father's side was Osmond Ardagh. He died young, before I was born. He worked as a civil servant in Africa. I learned from my grandmother that he had not really loved it. It was his duty more than his passion, also dictated by his parents. Recently I googled him. He had been a first-class cricketer at Oxford, but he only ever played one match as a professional cricketer before he left for Africa.

I am sure you can find similar stories among your own ancestors. The majority of people on this planet have a passion, a gift to give, but they spend their lives doing what is acceptable to other people.

We have to understand what it means to have your gift held back in this way. Think of a child you love, either your own, or a nephew or niece. Now imagine you go to the store and buy a gift for that child: the most special thing, something that would make that child's little heart explode with joy. Imagine wrapping that gift in shiny paper, with ribbons and bows. Now imagine hiding it in the back of the closet, behind the clothes, where it will not be discovered. Now imagine leaving it there. And leaving it. And leaving it. For months. For years. For decades. The child had some sense of the gift, but it never comes. I know this is an emotionally manipulative story to tell, but unfortunately, it is the story of many peoples' lives. They have an enormous gift that could make an impact on others' lives, but the gift is given occasionally as a trickle, not a torrent.

How to Discover Your Unique Gift

The best way to discover your unique gift is to ask the people who have known you for a long time. Ask your parents, your siblings, your childhood friends. You can ask your spouse or partner, your children. These are the people who have come to know you in the rough as well as the smooth; they have seen you vulnerable and without your make-up.

If you work with people, your clients are probably the least helpful people to ask. They may know your professional abilities, but they have probably not seen you in your relaxed innocence. The other least reliable person to ask is yourself. What we think we are here for is often so tied up with habits, addiction, narcissism, the avoidance of fear, and the attachment to pleasure, that asking other people is much more reliable.

The question to ask these people who know you well is along the lines of: "What are the qualities that you feel coming through me in a way that you don't feel quite the same with anybody else?" Find your own words. We are asking for qualities, not abilities. The kinds of answers you might get are: *"kind, bubbly, detail-oriented, inspiring, courageous...."* I usually suggest asking twelve people, by email, for twelve qualities each, making a total of 144.

Becoming clear about your unique gift may evoke a great deal of resistance. I have noticed that people often have more resistance about the thing they were born to do than anything else. The stakes are high. When you are working a nine-to-five job somewhere, not so much is on the line. People may appreciate you, they may not. Who gives a toss? When it is your true gift, you are much more vulnerable. Your guts are exposed. It is often terrifying to step into what you were born to do and into your true power. That is why as a coach I rely heavily on the opinion of people who know my clients well. You have too much invested in protecting yourself to see your own gift clearly.

I am a good example of this exploration. The people who have known me all my life tell me that the qualities they appreciate the most are clarity, eloquence, thinking outside the box, and being humorous. It is clear that my life-stream is very connected with being a teacher, with bringing forth spiritual awakening outside of the context of religious hierarchy. But you cannot imagine how much resistance I have had to being in this role. It means that I have to show up and live my life for real. My teacher in India originally commanded me to go and teach. I was very resistant. I had seen others become teachers, and I was not interested in attracting the kind of attention they received. I did it anyway for a while—he gave me no choice. After a few years, I went back to visit him and resigned. I told him I did not want to be in that role any longer.

He looked at me. He said nothing. He smiled.

Then he said: "Do whatever you want, but ultimately your destiny will win." He was right. Once you get a hint of the reason you are here in a body at this time, it will not leave you alone, however great is the resistance. But I needed him to see that in me, and bring it forth, just as I do now with my coaching clients.

Once you have a list of 144 qualities from the twelve people, you can start to correlate them. We use a spreadsheet for this. You will soon see that many of the words are similar; for example, "kind," "caring," "thoughtful," and "understanding." You can group such words together. And then you can organize your spreadsheet with the most popular ones at the top of the list. Some qualities will receive only one vote from one person: ignore those. Others will have ten or twelve votes: those are the ones to pay attention to. Once you have grouped and ordered them all in this way, look at the top five or six lines. This is a pretty good description of your unique gift, the song that only you can sing.

Are You Living it?

Once you have created this reading of your unique gift, from the reflection of the people close to you, it is time to compare it with how you live your life today. A good coach can help you to determine this.

When the correlation between the gift and how you spend most of your time is high, we can expect to see certain characteristics. You will be happy most of the time. You will probably find yourself being successful without effort. You will enjoy excellent health, because releasing resistance also reduces your stress level. You will most likely find yourself spending time with other people who are also giving their gift with nothing held back.

When there is a poor match between the unique gift and your daily life, we can expect to see the opposite. I would say that the most common cause of depression is suppressing your unique gift and doing things to make money that are not well suited to you. When the match is not good, everything in life becomes difficult. Your health will most likely decline, because the resistance to doing things that do not suit you is a major cause of stress.

I know people who have gone through a great deal of trauma and grief. Once of my older friends survived the Holocaust as a child. She saw both her parents die. But later in life she discovered how to express her deepest gifts, as a movie producer, and now she is one of the most contented people I know. She can look back on a life well lived.

The next step is to use your imagination. Take the top five or six qualities on your list, and start to think of people whose lives express these qualities. It could be people you know personally, celebrities or historical figures, or any mixture of these. One of my coaching clients had "warm, caring, a good listener, supportive, present" as her top qualities. She was working as a tax accountant when I met her, which was of course not the ideal way to express her gift. As models she chose Mother Theresa, her grandmother, a friend who was a nurse, and another friend who was a coach.

When there is a lot of resistance to living the gift, this step can be extremely difficult or even impossible to do without help. You may find yourself thinking only of models who died horrible deaths, went to prison, or had a strong shadow side. That is a way for the resistance to say, "Look this is impossible, or highly inadvisable." In contrast, when there is little resistance, you will find it easy to think of many shining examples of people living these qualities.

Once you have several solid examples of how these qualities can be and have been lived in real life, it is time to imagine a lifestyle that could express them in your own life. This could be a vocation or a career, or it could be a balance of several things, including work and play time. The woman I just mentioned also had "high sense of aesthetics and beauty" on her list. So, to imagine a life that included all of her qualities, she saw herself as a coach with a stunning office, who supported her clients to make their offices stunning, too. The important thing at this stage is to think outside of the box, so nothing gets excluded. In a coaching relationship, we take two weeks for this part of the process, during which the client sends in an update every day.

Now we can start the process to realign your life slowly, so that the way you spend your time is a clearer expression of your unique gift bundle. The key here is not to give up your day job at once, but to make gradual small changes. If you give up everything familiar and try to quickly launch a new career, it may evoke too much survival anxiety and be counter-productive. I know many people who abandoned stable incomes and careers to pursue a bigger vision, then had to retreat in disappointment and defeat when they hit unexpected barriers.

The art is to start with small steps. My tax-preparer client imagined a life for herself where she could support women to give their own gifts, and to create beautiful environments in the process. I asked her if there was one small step she could take in this direction during the next month. She decided to organize an evening for women in her area to come together, to connect, and to listen and support each other. It took a lot of preparation and planning to do this, but she pulled it off. It was not nearly such a hurdle to plan another evening, and then to make it a regular event. Adding this one element to her life made a huge difference. In Awakening Coaching we think of small changes that can be done in an hour or two a week, or as little as a few minutes a day. After some small victories, this amount of time can be increased to an hour or more a day, and you can add accepting donations or even charging fees. Over a year or two you may completely shift from the job you were doing before into something that completely expresses your true gift.

Meet Gordon

Let's see what's going on at the party now. See that man over there, singing with his guitar? Quite a group has gathered to hear him play. That's Gordon. I always take on a few coaching clients for free, and he was one of them. I met him in Santa Fe many years ago at a weekend seminar. He was in his mid-twenties and working on a building site. Look, he has finished his song, so he can tell you his story himself:

> When I went to that weekend, I had been hanging sheetrock all week. I remember my back was killing me. As usual. The pay was not so great in construction, and I had student loans, so I was a slave to the worksite. On the Sunday morning of the seminar I took in my guitar and played in the break. Arjuna, I remember you asked me to play for everyone. And then at the end of the weekend you offered to coach me for free. I was blown away.
>
> Music has always been my passion, as well as massage. I went to massage school after college, but I could not make it pay. So I ended up on building sites. Early on in the coaching, I remember Arjuna suggested I ask my boss if I could work four days a week and take Fridays off. He said yes. On those Fridays, I cleaned up my room the night before, and set up my massage table there. I invited friends to come for massages, just for free, because I loved it. Then Arjuna suggested putting out a donation bowl in the corner. If people liked the massage, they could put something in there. If not, they did not have to. I remember we did a lot of Radical Releasing around that time. I had a lot of fear and shame about asking for money. It took a few weeks to get to the point where I was booked every Friday. But I got there. Then Arjuna asked me to shift from a donation bowl to a fixed fee of $60 for each session. We had to do a bunch more Radical Releasing about that one. I had guys coming for massage from the building site. Even my boss came.

I also got a small recorder, called a Zoom, that made quite decent recordings. It had a built-in mic, and I could plug in my guitar with a cable. Each week Arjuna gave me the assignment to write one song, and to record it in the closet, among the clothes and the laundry. I did it. By the time we were done with the coaching I had most of a CD recorded in my closet, and I was working half the time with massage, and half on the site. My boss went along with it, as he was liking my massages.

Now it's been more than a year, and I don't work construction anymore. I play some gigs, I sell my CDs, and I have a pretty decent massage business. Mine is not a rags-to-riches story, but it is a sheetrock-dust-to-doing-what-I-love story. My back does not ache anymore, and I gotta say, I love my life and I love being me.

Spontaneous Creation

The last of the Innate Brilliances, which can allow anyone to become an excellent facilitator of awakening consciousness to anyone else, has to do with creation. Earlier we talked about Radical Releasing, which means to recognize the "frequencies" that we have been conditioned to resist, and which therefore persist. Very often these resisted frequencies define the quality and the story-line of our lives.

Spontaneous Creation is an advanced tool, which not everyone can use right away, because it requires steady access to limitless consciousness. Instead of dissolving resistance to frequencies, Spontaneous Creation is a way to create frequencies, out of nothing, that then become the blueprint of your external life.

Let us explore how this already works for you in your day-to-day life. We can think of any quality that most people desire: happiness is a good example. People have all sorts of different ideas about what a happy life should look like externally. We know what it is like to be happy, and we also know what it is like to be unhappy. Happiness is characterized by certain patterns of breathing, relaxation in the body, a good flow of energy, and a good flow of blood to the frontal cortex of the brain. These are physical qualities that can be measured. Happiness can also be recognized through certain emotions: feeling optimistic, upbeat, enthusiastic. Happiness also produces certain kinds of thoughts and beliefs. *I'm a good person with lots to contribute. I get along well with people. I have a great life and I'm grateful.* But deeper down, happiness is a frequency. It is a vibration that causes us to have certain kinds of thoughts, certain kinds of feelings, and certain kinds of activity in the body.

The most common way we try to create happiness is to acquire what we think of as the correct environment for happiness in our external lives. We try to buy the right house in the right area with the right kind of landscaping. Why? Because we think it will make us happy. We try to get married to the right partner, and then we strive to have the perfect number of children (I read somewhere that 2.35 was reported as the ideal number, which I guess means two normal sized children and one miniaturized version... but I digress). We think that the right family will make us happy. We want to have the right car, the right laptop computer; we want to go on vacation to the right places, because we have been led to believe that all of these things will create an experience of happiness.

In fact, as you and I well know from experience, all of these things are unstable. The house can develop dry-rot, your perfect spouse can have an affair with a neighbor, and once your children become teenagers they may not behave as angelically as you were hoping, even the smaller 0.35 member of the family. The laptop stops working, and then your call to Patel on tech support in India does not seem to solve the problem. You get the picture. Happiness based on changing external things is unstable.

There have been many books written lately about how to create happiness by changing your internal environment. Think the right thoughts, train yourself to have positive feelings, stay optimistic with a bright outlook, and say ten things you're grateful for every day. Although such practices really can help, we are still working in a Newtonian cause-and-effect universe, while quantum reality is also waiting to be explored.

We can best understand how Spontaneous Creation works by dabbling in the discoveries from quantum physics that have emerged in the last few decades. When we stay on the surface of things—table, chair, carpet, or even go a little deeper to raw materials or chemicals— things continue to behave in a predictable cause-and-effect way. It takes a lot of effort and energy to bring about change in a Newtonian universe. It is when we get down to the finer particles that make up atoms—electrons, quarks, bosons—that things become more interesting.

Way back in the 1920s, Werner Heisenberg postulated his famous "uncertainty principle," which states that you cannot accurately measure the position and momentum of any object at the same time. Once the implications of this theory were explored more deeply in laboratories by quantum physicists in the last decades, it generated the discovery of the "observer effect." Whenever you try to measure a subatomic particle, the very act of measurement causes it to have a location in space that it might not otherwise have. In other words, a subatomic particle such as an electron behaves as a wave until an observer measures it, and only then does it become a particle with a location in space. Everything is everywhere until you need it to be somewhere, and then it is the act of observation that gives it a location.

Spontaneous Creation works at the quantum level of creation, but instead of being an experiment performed by white-coated scientists in a physics laboratory, it happens in another laboratory: in your own consciousness, but buried deeper than the usual procession of thoughts, feelings, and bodily sensations. It also uses awareness to transform frequencies that are everywhere into experiences in time and space.

Spontaneous Creation was first described in the Yoga Sutras by Patanjali, who called it *Samyama*. It's a fairly easy process to describe, but a little more tricky to actualize, because it requires the capacity for attention to hover at very fine states of awareness. Here is how it works:

Step One. Relax into being Infinity. Practice Radical Awakening long enough that the attention is resting in a stable way as infinite consciousness. The best way to do this is to keep asking "Who is experiencing this moment?" and if any "thing" emerges as an answer, drop deeper to find out who is experiencing it.

If you want to have a really strong experience of Spontaneous Creation, a coach might continue working with you in this way for 20–30 minutes.

Step Two. Say a word internally. Once this infinite dimension of consciousness has opened up nicely, you could take a thought — a word — and think it very deliberately. In this case we will take the word "friendliness." We have experimented with using English words but also with using the same word in the coachee's native tongue. So Spanish people would do the process of Spontaneous Creation with *amistad*, a French person would use *convivialité*, etc. We have also experimented with using Sanskrit, which many people consider to be the first and original language, out of which all other languages have arisen. The word for friendliness in Sanskrit is *maitri*. You simply say the word to yourself a few times. You don't need to philosophically contemplate the true nature of friendliness: just say the word a few times silently to yourself.

Step Three. Drop the word into spaciousness. Now you drop the word into spaciousness. Imagine dropping a stone into a very deep well. This means you say the word "friendliness" and then completely relax into *being* infinite consciousness itself.

Step Four. Relax as spaciousness. Now just wait. Rest as spaciousness, with no expectation and no idea of what should happen next.

Step Five. I am going to leave step five as a surprise. You will experience that something happens. It is not something you do, it is spontaneous.

Try these steps on your own, and then you can log into the readers' website and tell us what happened.[24]

I just gave "friendliness" as an example, but you can use this process on many other qualities as well. For example, you can practice Spontaneous Creation with

---

[24] http://better-than-sex.kajabi.com/groups/9764

"compassion," "strength of an elephant," "clarity," or "focus." You can also practice Spontaneous Creation by visualizing certain objects and then dropping that visualization into spaciousness. Try doing Spontaneous Creation by visualizing another person's face, and then dropping that image into spaciousness. You can also try it by focusing on certain parts of your own body. Try doing this practice with the navel, or the pit of the throat, or different energy centers (known in India as *chakras*). Tune into different parts of your body for just a few moments and then drop each one into spaciousness.

It is fair to warn you that not everybody gets pristine results from Spontaneous Creation right away. I myself use this technique only in coaching with clients who have already realized all of the outcomes we set at the start of the coaching. Everything on the list of outcomes they had prepared for me has been accomplished: relationships are great, health is in balance, they have enough money, and it feels as if they really know and are living their unique gift. They might say to me, "On a scale from 1 to 10, my life is a 20." When someone gets to this point, the mental chatter becomes very quiet. The machine is no longer busy trying to figure out how to get more pleasure and less pain. Everything is just fine the way that it is. It is at this point that I guide my coaching clients into deeper and deeper dimensions of abiding as infinite consciousness, beyond "me" and "my story" completely, and I support them to create something out of nothing.

There is a little interesting catch to this, which I discovered when experimenting with my friend Jack Canfield, who co-authored the *Chicken Soup for the Soul* books. As you may know, Jack was one of the primary teachers in the movie *The Secret*, so he knows a lot about creation, intention, and the "Law of Attraction." Several years after that movie came out, he discovered something very interesting. If you set an intention that is focused on your own needs and desires and then test the strength of it, using applied kinesiology, the results are fairly weak. If you set another intention that is for the well-being not only of yourself but also your family, your friends, or your tribe, your core-body strength becomes much stronger. If you test a third time and set an intention for the well-being of all of humanity or all sentient beings, the strength of the body while thinking of the intention is much greater. You can watch Jack and myself testing this on the readers' website.[25]

After experimenting in this way with Jack, we brought the same testing to Spontaneous Creation. And lo and behold, we found exactly the same thing that Jack had discovered using applied kinesiology. When you use Spontaneous Creation on a quality that is applied to your own life, such as happiness, focus, or strength, it definitely brings results, but there are limits. If you now go back and practice Spontaneous Creation focused on another person—for example, you could visualize a friend who has been having financial troubles—and hold the image of their face in awareness while mentally saying the word "gratitude" or "abundance" and drop it into spaciousness, the results are more startling. This is a form of blessing or benediction. If you now go back to Spontaneous Creation and think about a much bigger predicament, such as a war happening somewhere, or you evoke an image of the global banking crisis, and then hold the word "sanity" in awareness, the subjective experience of Spontaneous Creation is even stronger.

When we talked about the other Innate Brilliances, I introduced you to someone else at the party who could tell you about their experience. I hope you found that helpful. For this last Brilliance I'm not going to do that. I feel I've already given you too much of a hint of where all of this may lead, and I don't want to spoil it by leading you to foregone conclusions. Experiment with Spontaneous Creation on your own, see what happens, and then report the results on the readers' website, or you could hook up with a Certified Awakening Coach and explore Spontaneous Creation together.

---

[25] http://better-than-sex.kajabi.com/posts/testing-the-power-of-intentions

Talking about hooking up with a coach, I'd like to tell you a little more now about what a coaching relationship looks like in real life. There are many different coaching schools and each works in its own way. So we are going to focus on what happens in the relationship between a coach and a coachee using Awakening Coaching, and hopefully the principles will be useful to you whether you want to explore our particular method or not.

Doing It

CHAPTER 13

Getting Coached

I know you came to the party with some curiosity. Let's go sit down together for a few minutes and think about how all of this might apply to you. There are hundreds of approaches to coaching available today. Each has its strengths and special gifts to offer. If you are thinking about getting coached, I suggest you interview coaches from several different backgrounds to find the perfect fit for you.

I am going to tell you here about the relationship you would enter into with a coach in Awakening Coaching. In many ways, this will be similar to other approaches; in some ways, it may be unique. If you plan to get coached, it may offer a good reference point for comparing coaching methods. If you are already a coach or you plan to become one, it may give you some ideas of how to tweak your relationship with potential and current clients.

Not Everyone Is "Coachable"

I want to come clean with you and acknowledge that not everybody is equally suited to being coached. Coaching is a particular kind of relationship that works really well for some kinds of people, and not for others. Let us talk about the kind of person who is highly "coachable."

Many years ago I was interviewing my friend Gay Hendricks for a course I was putting together. He said something that felt so perfect, I don't think I could say it in any better words.

> *You lose interest in your defenses, after a while, after running through them 5,800 times, and finally you realize there's nothing left to defend. At that point, things dissolve.*

For almost all of us, we have tried to improve the quality of our lives by changing external things. We have tried to find the right partner; we have tried to find the perfect house with the perfect neighbors in the perfect community. We have tried to eat the right foods to have perfect health. We have tried to make enough money to pay for this perfect life. There comes a point for many people, but not for everybody, where all of that effort starts to seem pointless. When you have rearranged the furniture enough times, and you have still not found the fulfillment you long for, you might want to try not another rearrangement but a different space in which to live.

For many of us, we then shift to a more internal inquiry. We recognize that we have emotions, reactive feelings, and beliefs that determine the quality of our lives. We try to shift negative feelings into positive feelings. We try to change dysfunctional beliefs into the kind of thoughts that will get us what we want. But that process also can lead to a dead end.

When you have run out of options for changing things, either external or internal, an approach to coaching that emphasizes shifting consciousness may become interesting for you. Such an approach is tailor-made for someone with a deep intuition of their true potential as limitless, as humorous, as radiant, and outside the game.

You may have felt inspired by experiencing that dimension in another person. Or you may have had moments in your life where you touched into it just enough that it would not leave you alone again. Most people who have such moments of inspiration find that the access to awakening is fleeting. It might come through meditation, being on a retreat, engaging in extreme sports, or having sex. But it disappears again, leaving you grasping for more.

A good Awakening Coach offers you reliable support to come back to spaciousness, again and again, and to learn how to recognize that as constantly available, just beneath the noise of day-to-day life.

You may also find yourself curious about how those brief moments of expansion, of well-being and humor, can be integrated more easily into every area of your life. How can your relationships become more authentic? How can the work you do in the world become a play where money is a spontaneous byproduct? How can your parenting become a vehicle for something greater than just passing on your own prejudices to another generation?

This is very different from the field of self-improvement, or even healing. It is an investigation into how to step out of your own way and allow something beyond the story of "Me" to have its way. A coach cannot give you that thirst. Nor can the coach supply you with the determination to break through old habits into something new and different. A coach can support and encourage you, from a place of Inspired Certainty, once the thirst is there.

This style of coaching is probably *not* a good fit for you if:

- You feel that you carry a deep sense of wounding from your childhood or other past trauma that is painful and overwhelming. In such circumstances, a licensed psychotherapist would be better suited to help you.

- It is important to you right now to make a lot of money, or to reach a new goal with your company, or to learn how to snag a date more effectively. There are other methods of coaching and support that are much more effective at creating those specific outcomes.

- You are suffering from a deep-rooted physical condition. Although Awakening Coaching can definitely support you in experiencing the conditions in consciousness that set up those physical ailments, we are not doctors and we do not heal, treat, prescribe, or cure. To work directly with illness in the body, you need to be in touch with a licensed healthcare professional.

- You feel severely depressed, anxious, obsessive compulsive, or paranoid in a way that is debilitating to you. These can be symptoms of mental illness, and carry an unnecessary stigma in our society. Mental illness can be treated and cured in just the same way that many physical illnesses can. But we are not the right people for that. It is smart to seek out the services of a psychiatrist or psychologist when that is called for.

- Someone wants you to experience coaching, but you don't feel a lot of resonance from your own side. That person might even offer to pay the tab for you. This is not like getting a massage, where you lie back and have it done to you. You need to be actively participating; you need to be motivated and involved. So if someone else is providing the motivation and you are just along for the ride, it probably will not be very effective.

- You feel a strong allegiance to a particular belief system, which you hold as sacred and beyond questioning. In Awakening Coaching, we are not out to confront you, but it is important to be able to question anything and everything in order to come home truly to yourself.

The Structure of the Relationship

I am going to describe to you now, somewhat briefly, the way that a relationship unfolds between Awakening Coaches and their clients. This may be useful information, if you would like to experience Awakening Coaching for yourself. It might be equally interesting if you work with other methods, to suggest to you a model that could work well for you, too.

Step 1. The Orientation Interview

The first relevant step for you is to find out how Awakening Coaching could impact you personally. You can ask any Awakening Coach for a free 20–30 minute interview, to explore what it is that you hope to get out of a coaching relationship. During this interview, the coach will ask you powerful and relevant questions to find out where you would like to be, and what you would like your life to look like, at the end of a coaching relationship. There is no censorship or limit to the answers that you can come up with. They might be "spiritual." They might be relational, financial, or career-oriented. The outcomes might be connected to your health or why you are on the planet. Your coach will be able to evaluate, in as honest a way as possible, if they are really in a position to help you. They can consider whether these particular outcomes are realistic for Awakening Coaching within an eight to twelve week period. They can consider if they have had success with similar outcomes with previous clients. They can consider whether their own life experience gives them the Inspired Certainty to support you, and to know that there is hope at the end of the journey. At the end of the conversation you will have the opportunity to create together whatever financial arrangement you both choose in entering into a coaching relationship.

Step 2. Hiring Your Coach

If you decide to go ahead and enter into a relationship with a coach, it is a commitment, not unlike getting married (for a little while), or signing up for a course at a college. It requires commitment on both sides. Your coach will send you a welcome letter explaining exactly how the coaching relationship will unfold, as well as a more detailed questionnaire to complete. You have several days to do this.

Step 3. The First Session.

In your first session with an Awakening Coach, you explore the questionnaire that you completed. You are going to focus together on four really important questions:

- **What is your deepest longing?** What are your aspirations, hopes, and dreams? These are big-picture questions, and do not need to be practical at all. Your coach wants to know the ultimate driving purpose for your life, whether you actually get there or not. What would it take for your life to be a 100 out of 10? Would it mean making an Oscar-winning movie? Would it mean sitting for years, unmoving on a mountain top, hearing only the sound "Om" between your temples? Would it mean deeply, and without distraction, loving a partner with nothing held back? These are not things that you hope to accomplish during the coaching series. These are the most ambitious goals for your entire life.

- **What gets in the way?** Your coach will want to know the main habits that interfere with you living your deepest vision and purpose. These might be things such as procrastination, irritability, laziness, getting emotionally reactive at inappropriate moments....

- **What are your strengths?** It is important to take inventory on the places where you are already strong and reliable. For example, if you always keep your word, no matter what the circumstances, this would be regarded as a pre-existing strength. If you have been meditating for 40 years and it is not a challenge for you to go back to the mediation cushion every day, this would also be considered a strength. A daily practice of yoga, going to the gym, being really honest with the people around you, being kind and generous: these are all strengths that you may have developed through previous disciplines.

- **What are the specific outcomes** you want to get out of this coaching series? This will revisit the ground you covered in the initial interview, but now put into context with more refinement and clarity. Together with your coach, you are going to come up with eight or ten specific outcomes for what you want your life to look like at the end of the relationship. Your coach will do everything within their power to help you realize those outcomes.

At the end of the first session, your coach is going to give you your first Empowerment Practices, as we have already talked about. As you may remember, Empowerment Practices are really short interventions you can bring to your life that usually just take a few minutes at a time, to shift your habits from automatic behavior that no longer serves you to new habits that are creative and fresh, and bring out parts of you that may have been hidden.

Step 4. Send the Daily Report

Between sessions, you have the opportunity to send your coach a daily report. This is very short and should take no more than a few minutes to complete each day. In the report, you let your coach know whether you did each of the Empowerment Practices, if so for how long, and what the outcome was. There is no right or wrong answer within a daily report. You just tell the truth. If, for example, you miss a particular practice every day for a week, that gives your coach the useful information that this practice is too challenging or that you have hit a solid wall of resistance. If, on the other hand, you report that another practice is incredibly easy for you but has very little impact, your coach knows that the practice needs to be tweaked to become a little more challenging and interesting.

As has been discussed already, these daily practices are absolutely essential to the coaching process. If you are able to do practices every day and report on them, you can witness miracles between one session and the next. If you rely only upon sessions with your coach, and her or him to do all the work, your progress through coaching will not seem as significant.

Step 5. Subsequent Sessions

You are going to meet with your coach every two weeks for at least ninety minutes each time. Your coach will use all of the tools that we have described earlier, and may bring in many other tools as well that I have not had the opportunity to share with you here today. The way that these intermediate sessions unfold is a very intuitive dance that you enter into together. Moreover, as you explore the Empowerment Practices every day, you are going to open up new areas of availability and potential evolution. Your coach can meet you in that availability and bring out those gifts that were previously hidden.

Often your coach will invite you to have additional contact between sessions, depending on what you write in your daily reports. Sometimes a coach will do Radical Releasing with you every day for a period, if that is needed, to help you break through a particular block. Sometimes the coach will speak to you for a few minutes on the phone to adjust the practices so they continue to be exciting and interesting but not overwhelmingly stressful.

Step 6. Completing the Series

By the end of your coaching series, which may extend to eight, ten, or twelve weeks, all of the outcomes you listed should have been handled. This means not that you will never experience these challenges in your life again, but that you know how to handle them in a way that can be creative and humorous. For example, you might sometimes get into a really bad mood, where you feel irritable and critical of everybody around you. It would be unrealistic to promise that you are never going to have that feeling again, and in fact that would be a restriction on your freedom. Instead, your coach can promise to guide you to completely dissolve the resistance to what you are feeling, and show you ways to be with those feelings when they arise, so that instead of shutting you down or damaging your connection with other people, they can actually become a foundation for deeper intimacy, humor, and aliveness.

Above all, it is really important to understand that coaching is a collaborative relationship. Just as in sports, the athlete has to show up in uniform, ready to play ball, and the coach needs to show up inspired and ready to call forth the fullest potential of the athlete. If the athlete were not to show up for the game, to show up drunk or under the influence of a drug, or be caught up in other personal drama, of course the capacity of a sports coach would be limited. Awakening Coaching is very similar. Your coach can help you to deal with resistance when it arises, but at the same time, you need to willing to be an active participant in moving towards the outcomes you want.

When both the coach and the coachee are fully committed to the adventure of evolution, there are really no limits to the miracles that are possible. I'd love to share with you some of the outcomes that clients have brought to the coaching relationship, and that have been resolved through this process. Let's do that now.

CHAPTER 14

Specific Applications

We have talked about how a coach can support you in specific outcomes you would like from a coaching relationship. Let's take time now to look at examples of what these outcomes might be, and where this kind of coaching has been effective in the past.

Relaxing More Deeply in the Natural State

What makes this style of coaching distinct from others is the emphasis on knowing who you are, outside the story, then resolving practical things in the rest of your life from that clarity. We have talked about Radical Awakening, a series of questions that can guide a client back to resting in the natural state of consciousness. But it is the Inspired Certainty of the coach, asking the right questions, that can make the most difference to dissolving doubt. A coach can continually remind you that what you intuitively seek is who you already are, your true nature.

For example, Brian had long considered himself a "spiritual seeker." He had taken courses in Vipassana meditation, lived in ashrams, and studied with several teachers. But his life had been about attaining peak states, and trying to hold onto them forever, which he labeled "Enlightenment." For eight weeks of Awakening Coaching, he went through Radical Awakening many times, to come back to the recognition of what is already here in this moment. Every day he wrote down all his beliefs about what makes this moment incomplete: *there is something missing, not enough, I'm not going to make it, I'm not good enough.* He did Radical Releasing on them all. By the end of the series, his spiritual ambitions had not been fulfilled: they had dissolved. He could no longer find proof of anything missing in this moment.

Tailor-Made Practice

Carol learned meditation from an Indian teacher in the 1970s, when she was in her early twenties. The teacher spoke about her reaching higher states of consciousness in a few years, with regular meditation twice a day. She went on retreats, learned yoga postures, studied texts, did long fasts, and changed her diet. For many years she worked for this teacher's organization and had no dealings with money. She came to Awakening Coaching in her fifties. Not only was her hair grey: so were her clothes, so was her skin. She was very serious and had deeply engrained habits.

Carol was coached by another woman, who gently introduced her to tailor-made practice. Slowly she opened to the possibility that some of the things she had been doing were not ideally suited to her disposition. She started to dance. She deepened friendships with other women. She changed her hair, wore brighter clothes. Her feelings started to flow again. She cried, she got angry, she came alive. I met her again six months later. I could have sworn she was the daughter of the earlier Carol. She had replaced a one-size-fits-all approach with one that suited her needs and disposition.

Jacob found great difficulty in getting things done. His job had flexible hours, so he could get up in the middle of the morning and go to bed in the middle of the night. He felt he had lost his sense of direction and purpose. His girlfriend made all the decisions for both of them.

Jacob also worked with tailor-made practices, but quite different from Carol's. After Radical Releasing sessions, his coach suggested adopting a regular schedule and getting up half an hour earlier each day. Jacob started to practice regular Chi Kung, and silent meditation, sitting with a straight spine. He made lists of small objectives for each day, sending reports to his coach.

Jacob and Carol demonstrate that one person's food is another person's poison. Coaching can be a great way to receive practices tailor-made for you.

Finding Your Mate

Trisha had been single for eight years. In her late thirties, she often despaired that she would ever find a mate. She also deeply regretted never having had children. Her way of dealing with this missing aspect of her life was to sink herself into corporate work, which entailed twelve-hour work days. She had accumulated many crusty beliefs: *men are not to be trusted, they use women for their own ends,* and *love will never last.* Her previous relationships "proved" these beliefs to be accurate.

Almost all Trisha's coaching was oriented to her longing to love and be loved by a man. Her coach gave her practices to support her to open her heart and feel vulnerable again—a great challenge. She did the "Feeling Rainbow" practice[26] twice a week, danced every day, and followed other practices to enhance feminine energy. Trisha also did Radical Releasing around her residual beliefs about men. Her coach gave her practices to spend time with other people. She developed new friendships with women, with the specific emphasis on not talking about work, money, or career. This was a great challenge for her, too.

Toward the end of the coaching series she took a two-week vacation with her sisters, for the first time since she was a child. All these practices brought her more into her feminine energy. Slowly, hardly noticeably at first, her relationship with men changed. By the end of the series she was not magically married or engaged, but she felt very different about herself. She had no doubts that she is an attractive woman, that she has love to share with the lucky man. Thirteen months after she started coaching, Trisha did become engaged.

---

[26] http://better-than-sex.kajabi.com/posts/the-feeling-rainbow

The Deeper Love

Mark and Donna wanted coaching together as a couple, as the light had gone out of their marriage. She was much more motivated than he was to participate, but he came along anyway, like a bored teenager. They were convinced all their problems would be easily solved if the other partner changed. She wanted him to open up and share his feelings, to pay more attention to her, to be more romantic. He said he was tired of her creating endless dramas, of feeling criticized. Chameli and I understood they had only been occupying a tiny corner of the mansion of their potential intimacy.

They started to use a practice we call "Here-Nowing."[27] It is a simple way, for a few minutes a day, to practice pure listening and pure honesty. We asked them to give five appreciations to each other throughout the day, whether they felt these were real or not. We also guided them to practice open-eyed meditation together: to sit facing one another for twenty to thirty minutes without speaking, looking softly into the left eye of the other. For conservative professionals in their fifties, this was a new experience.

After two weeks they reported that, after decades of marriage, they each had come to recognize they did not know each other well. So many sides had been buried or ignored. Once we had ignited their curiosity, we took them in a direction that felt counter-intuitive to both of them. The practices we had started with were intended to cultivate intimacy and merging. Now we gave them practices to cultivate polarity.

We suggested they see each for no more than an hour a day. Then we worked with each partner individually, learning about the passions and interests that had been forgotten or buried over the years. Donna loved to be outside, to walk in nature, and was frustrated with Mark's lack of interest in that. We

---

[27] http://better-than-sex.kajabi.com/posts/here-nowing--2

encouraged her to walk with other friends, or alone. Mark joined a men's group and rediscovered his interest in old motorbikes. He hooked up with an old friend, and they talked about restoring a bike that had sat in the shed for twenty years. Mark and Donna had one date a week during this part of the coaching. We encouraged them to go somewhere they had never been before and to dress in unfamiliar ways. After several weeks, they could practice the vital art of alternating polarizing and merging, and their marriage came alive again.

Healing Old Relationships

Cheryl was working in the Hollywood film industry. Seemingly, she had it all. Her profile on IMDb was impressive, she had more money than she knew what to do with, and she was in excellent health. Cheryl was empowered, creative, smart, and funny ... except for the eight or ten times a day she received a phone call from her mother, or for Sundays, which were devoted to obligatory family gatherings. Then Cheryl became a surly teenager, boiling with resentments she could neither express nor let go of. She wanted coaching because she experienced herself as trapped in her teens.

The coaching started with Radical Awakening, as well as practices to stabilize access to awakening. She needed to develop an expanded perspective on her personal story before there was any chance of shifting it. Cheryl did a number of dialogs with her mother, but not in person. She closed her eyes and met her mother where she was causing Cheryl the most trouble: in her own imagination. She went through a process we call "Dissolving Separation." Within herself, Cheryl would tell her mother things she had not said before, and then listen to her mother's responses. After a few minutes of going back and forth like this, Cheryl was able to shift her attention and become her mother. She could feel the thoughts, feelings, and even physical contractions that were keeping her mother trapped in obsessive control. By the end of the coaching relationship, Cheryl could, for the first time, experience compassion for her mother, and meet her as an adult. The coaching also focused on her career, and she went on to her most important project ever.

Conscious Parenting

When David and Samantha divorced, their daughter Luna was only four. The process seemed amicable, except that after he got his own place, David had to learn how to be a dad as a solo act. He had Luna every other weekend, as well as some weeknights. Up to now, they had been a threesome, and David had never realized the importance of Sam's presence in the dynamic. Luna was reluctant to spend time with her father. She hardly spoke during her visits, and asked frequently when she could "go home." David fell back on the unconscious parenting habits he had inherited from his own father: he became authoritarian, and tried to modify Luna's behavior by bribing her with treats or withholding things she liked. That just made matters worse.

David's coaching began without addressing the dynamic with his daughter directly. Instead, his coach worked to deepen and strengthen his masculine presence. David experienced Radical Awakening many times, and began a daily morning practice of Chi Kung. After several weeks, he began to experience a reservoir of energy and well-being in his lower belly. Now, still not attending to the dynamic with his daughter directly, David's coach encouraged him to experiment with "giving the energy" through his whole body to other people. Once he could feel this was effective, he started to bring this conscious masculine presence to his relationship with his daughter. When Luna was upset, rebellious, or hyperactive, rather than using words, David brought his presence to parenting. The next step of the coaching, from this deeper conscious presence, was to meet Luna where she was. David was encouraged to get down on the floor as much as possible and play with Luna on her own terms. His daughter taught him how to play, how to feel, how to experience wonder, and how to have fun. By the end of ten weeks of coaching, father and daughter had become close, and Luna looked forward equally to the time she spent with each of her parents.

The Unique Gift

Brian was an Australian hedge-fund manager, living in New York. His annual income was enough to retire on for life. He had all the best toys, a spacious penthouse loft overlooking Manhattan, and he was engaged to be married. But instinctively he knew he was not living the life he was born to live. Brian's coach took him through the process for discovering his unique gift. Brian asked twelve friends to suggest twelve qualities; they were compiled into a list and compared with his current life. Needless to say, many of the qualities were not being expressed.

Halfway through the coaching series, Brian's coach suggested he take a five-day solitary retreat. Brian went away to a cabin, with no writing materials, no reading, no cell phone, and no Internet access. He was asked not to do vigorous exercise or any spiritual practice, like meditation. He was just to wait, patiently, for insight to come. This is a great practice, particularly for men, to rediscover clarity and sense of purpose. When Brian got back from the retreat, everything was clear to him. He realized he was not really in love with his fiancée, and was holding them both back from happiness. Gracefully, kindly, he broke off the engagement. He gave up his job at the hedge fund; he let go of his apartment, his car, and all his toys. He moved back to Australia, and to his greatest love: surfing. Within a year, by following this passion he developed a new company with friends that revolved around his love of water sports. He made a fraction of the money he had before, but he found his real gift again.

Making Big Decisions

Michael had worked in the same company, as a sales executive, for more than ten years. The base salary plus commissions were more than enough to keep his young family in a comfortable lifestyle. So when one of the company's founders left to form his own startup and invited Michael to be a partner, he was thrown into a chaos of mental indecision. The enormous opportunity of this offer would not let him rest, while at the same time, letting go of his financial stability seemed too risky.

Michael's coach guided him through several sessions of "Stacking Radical Releasing." They talked for half an hour about Michael's predicament, and the coach wrote down each and every point of view he heard Michael say about the situation. The coach also noted the opposites of these points of view, as well as points of view implied but not articulated. Once Michael's coach had accumulated a list of 30 or 40 points of view, they practiced Radical Releasing, on one point of view after another, so each of them lost the charge, becoming neutral and empty. They continued like this until there were no charge statements left relevant to Michael's indecision. When a coach guides someone through many layers of Radical Releasing in this way, it brings the client to a state we call "Clear Seeing." The client no longer has charged opinions about the topic, and is able to see things clearly, and to be more sensitive to, and in touch with, the natural flow of life.

At the end of the sessions, Michael realized no decision was needed immediately. He discovered a trust that the right time for action would come. That time did come, when the startup company received unexpected funding. Then Michael knew exactly what to do, without having to think about it. This is one of the practical consequences of coming to Clear Seeing: that indecision evaporates, and it becomes clear what to do, and what not to do, in every moment.

Honoring the Body

Charlotte had been experiencing unexplained symptoms in her body for over a year: low energy, occasional rashes, and irregularities in her menstrual cycle. She had been to every kind of allopathic, naturopathic, Ayurvedic, and Chinese medical practitioner she could find. Each practitioner had a theory; each had supplements and treatments to offer. But nothing changed the mysterious bundle of symptoms that plagued her. Charlotte was a student in the Awakening Coaching Training, so she received her coaching as part of her own preparation to become a coach.

Her coach led her into a process of dialoguing with her own body. She had been unaware how out of touch she had been with the physical animal of the human body. Now Charlotte was able to speak to her body, while in deep relaxation. She could ask her body, "How are you? What you need? How can I support you?"

At first she received little response. That was no surprise: the body was behaving like a dog or a horse that had been mistreated for years. It was weary of contact with the human mind. But slowly, as Charlotte practiced these dialogues, her body became more conversational. She discovered that her body does not speak German (her native tongue), nor does it speak English or any other language. The body communicates through physical sensations. And it began to talk to her. As she asked her body questions, she would receive visceral responses. If she asked her body about certain foods, kinds of exercise, or when it wanted to sleep and for how long, she felt waves of energy, some contracted and fearful, some flowing and pleasurable. In this way she discovered, for example, that her body did not do well with sugar or milk. It was requesting much more time to rest and play; it particularly liked to be in warm water. It was easy for her coach to suggest practices that Charlotte could report on, based on the information that came in the sessions. In only eight weeks her symptoms cleared up, and Charlotte was also living a different kind of life.

Finding the Ideal Weight

Maria had struggled with her weight since she first had children, forty years ago. She had managed to lose tens of pounds on many occasions, through various diets, or juice fasting. But the weight always came back. Maria took great pride in cooking, which was her primary way to bond with her husband and her children, the youngest of whom was now a college student. Everybody loved Maria for what she created in the kitchen. It was her identity. Because she was around food so much of the day, the temptation was right in front of her to snack and to taste all the good things she was making, supposedly for other people.

Through coaching she discovered all the things she was avoiding feeling by eating when she was not hungry. With her coach, she made a long list of the "frequencies" she did not want to experience. At the top of the list was: "I am ugly." Maria was caught in a vicious cycle. The more she felt she was not beautiful, the more she wanted to avoid experiencing this difficult feeling, and the most effective way she knew to avoid feeling it was to eat. She did Radical Releasing on all the frequencies she did not want to feel. Then she reached the point where "I am beautiful" and "I am ugly" were both without charge. As she untangled all these frequencies, avoided for decades, her identity shifted. Her relationship with her family changed as she discovered she could show up as a loving, interesting, and desirable woman without having to bake a cake to prove it.

Maria developed an interest in raw-food diets, and became an expert raw-food chef. She started each day with a green smoothie, made mostly of green leafy vegetables, with a few fruits to sweeten the taste. At first, her husband and teenage son thought she was crazy. They would make nauseated faces if she even asked them to try her new dishes. But, because her identity was no longer wrapped up in gaining approval through her cooking, she stayed with her new interest. She still cooked for her family, but also provided raw-food alternatives. It took some time, but eventually they became curious about her new lifestyle. She lost weight, but through a gradual embracing of a healthy lifestyle, rather than a quick diet. She learned to love her body as it is. She and her husband became more sexual, after more than forty years of marriage. Now Maria has graduated as a coach, and she loves to support other women to make friends with their body, and to adopt healthy lifestyles and diets.

Making Money

Peter's greatest resentment in life was having to deal with money. For more than twenty years he had been enthusiastic about the idea of "financial freedom." He had been involved in every kind of multilevel marketing scheme, every new investment opportunity, as well as futures on the stock market, and currency trading. He was convinced that if he could only create financial freedom, he could lead the life he was born to live. Ironically, his day-to-day finances were constantly in upheaval, and he spent huge amounts of energy thinking about money.

As he talked with his coach, it became clear that Peter had multiple conflicting points of view about money. He loved it, he craved it, as much as he hated it and wanted to keep it out of his life. He envied people who were rich as much as he despised them. This complex web of conflict led Peter to be frozen about money. He did many sessions of Stacking Radical Releasing, where he and his coach worked on multiple resisted frequencies, one after another.

The most important thing that shifted everything for Peter was the conscious and deliberate practice of gratitude. His coach sent him to a website called globalrichlist.com, where Peter could see where he stood financially relative to the rest of the world. His coach suggested that as Peter went to sleep each night, he list all the things he had been grateful for that day. Some were obvious: things he already appreciated. But some were things he had taken for granted, like access to clean water, having a variety of clothes to wear, and being able to eat food grown in another part of the world and flown to Germany for him to enjoy.

His coach guided Peter away from money cravings and into deep appreciation and gratitude for the things he already had.

Peter began to instill the world "enough" into his vocabulary. He realized that he had enough food, enough books, a big enough car, enough entertainment, enough clothes, and certainly enough things to do. Aside from his mind's fixation on more more more, he had enough money.

Through relaxing into gratitude, Peter's energy and attention shifted from wanting more money to doing what he loved. Peter had always been an artist, a writer, and a musician. But those activities didn't adequately support his craving for financial freedom. As he realized that he already had enough of everything, he could focus attention on the things he loved doing, and to his surprise, his passions made him money. By the end of coaching, he was not the multimillionaire he had wanted to be. But he could honestly say that money was no longer an issue, because he always had enough for what he needed right now. And he found ways to use his considerable talents to help people way less fortunate than him in other parts of the world.

Birthing a Creative Project

Stephan had invented something radically new that could change the computing industry dramatically. He knew it was huge, and he had courted the attention of some of the world's biggest technology companies. He had taken out international patents. He knew what he had created not only had immense environmental integrity, but also would save immense amounts of time and money for companies and personal computer users.

Stephan was on the brink of success. Tens of millions of dollars were ready to be exchanged. Production could begin quickly. He simply had to finish a detailed proposal for the investment to be locked in place. Yet Stephan was stuck. Every time he sat down at his computer to write, he was plagued by a torrent of other things he needed to do urgently. Days would go by without any progress on the document.

Stefan came to coaching to break through his block. Quickly he discovered, with his coach, that he was as terrified of his project being successful as he was desirous of it. He did a lot of Radical Releasing on the resisted frequencies around material and creative success.

The most important breakthrough for Stephan was when he experienced Radical Awakening. Having a background in technology and business, he had never been interested in spiritual practice before. So when his coach guided him into the recognition of the dimension of the mind that is limitless, it was both a shock and an epiphany to Stephan to know himself as boundary-less, beyond definition and free. His coach guided Stephan to rest in this limitless consciousness frequently throughout the day, a few minutes at a time.

Every time Stephan wanted to write, his coach guided him to return to this infinite consciousness. Stephan learned to hover with attention as this infinite consciousness, and to become sensitive to the fine impulses of creativity that are being born at that finest state of mental activity. He came to realize that the invention he had called "his" was not really his at all. It had been birthed through him, but he was more of a vehicle than an owner. Then, in his writing sessions, he became more of a scribe than an author. The whole activity became lighter, easier and fun. Stefan was able to complete and deliver the document before the coaching ended. I have changed his name for the purpose of this book, but the invention that came through Stephan has now been produced and is almost certainly affecting your life.

So many people have written books, completed CDs, brought new inventions and companies to the market, and finished other creative projects through Awakening Coaching. Whereas mysticism has traditionally focused on renouncing the world, modern mysticism finds its full blossoming in giving everything to the world as a creative gift.

CHAPTER 15

Becoming a Coach

A s we have been talking together about the possibilities of coaching, it may be that you have realized your interest lies more in becoming a coach to others rather than, or as well as, receiving coaching yourself.

There are many wonderful coaching schools today all over the world. Each has its own particular flavor. Each attracts students for its particular method, and each has its own training track. There is no government-issued license for coaching, so each school provides its own certification. Coaches can also be certified by the International Coach Federation, founded by Thomas J. Leonard in 1995. If you feel drawn to becoming a coach, I encourage you to investigate many different schools before settling on a final choice. It may also be wise to train with more than one school, so as to obtain a variety of tools for different kinds of clients.

The great thing about training to be a coach is that it is relatively quick and easy. Consider the difference between a trainer at the gym and a knee surgeon. My son recently trained to be an instructor in CrossFit, a method of personal fitness that has been sweeping the world like wildfire. He was able to learn the basics of how to instruct others in one weekend. Of course, to become a good personal trainer you would spend longer on it, but nothing like the eight or ten years it would require to take your pre-med as an undergraduate, go through med school, do an internship, and finally train as a surgeon. The reason is that training to work with healthy people, encouraging them to reach their peak performance, is much easier and more straightforward than learning how to work with injury or illness.

In just the same way, training to become a coach is much easier, simpler, and quicker than training to become a psychotherapist or psychiatrist. An important part of the training is knowing when you should refer your clients to a licensed professional.

Three Good Reasons to Become a Coach

If you want to know specifics about our school, I'll tell you where to find them a little later. But for now let's talk about training as a coach in more general terms.

I am aware of three good and valid reasons why someone might consider taking a coaching training. There is no hierarchy of merit in these. Each is perfectly right for a particular person.

The first reason to train to become a coach is because you love the idea of receiving support from your peers and supporting them in turn. In our context, which focuses on the embodiment of awakening, you might have found yourself tired of hierarchical spirituality: of guru-centered organizations, with rules, and membership, and a predictable vocabulary and way of behaving. You might be burning to leave the well-trodden path and take a hike into the unexplored wilderness with a group of courageous friends. This may have little to do with how you make money. You might be happy as a film maker, or an executive, or an artist, or a mother who stays at home to look after her kids. Your interest in coaching is the peer support. About one-third of the people who train with us fall into this category.

The second good and valid reason to train to become a coach is because you want to integrate the tools taught in a particular coaching school into an existing profession. In our school, for example, we train many psychiatrists, psychologists, doctors, and counselors to become proficient in the basic skills of Radical Awakening, Radical Releasing, and Embodiment Practices. These people will probably never hang up a shingle as Certified Awakening Coaches. They will continue quietly with their chosen profession. They frequently report that, once they have tools to help their patients access infinite consciousness, the results are staggeringly more effective. Dr. Marc Loewer, for example, is a psychiatrist practicing in Germany. He was a psychiatrist before he trained with us, he is a psychiatrist now, and he plans to continue being a psychiatrist for the rest of his long and glorious life. He reports that the tools he has learned with us have allowed him to be more present with his patients and, when appropriate, to help his patients bypass their personal story—often of suffering, defeat, and self-doubt—and discover the dimension of themselves that was never broken. Approximately half of the people who train in our school fall into this second category. They are not looking for a new career, but instead want to bring powerful and effective tools to enhance the career they already have.

The third good and valid reason to train as a coach is because you want to start a new career. You may have become tired of being a sheep farmer, a hairdresser, or a nuclear physicist, and you want to do something new and different. In this scenario, of course, you need to take the training a little more seriously, devote more time to it, and probably do more courses. I would strongly suggest that you think about training with at least two different schools if you want to be a professional coach, so that you have a nice variety of skills to offer your coaching clients. In our school, it is certainly not everybody who wants to follow this route: perhaps one in five or even less. When someone makes the decision that they want to be a full-time coach using our method, I invite them to join an apprenticeship program, where they work with me closely for a year, mastering all the skills they need to deal with any and every circumstance, both with individuals and in groups.

What Kinds of Qualities Would Make a Good Full-time Coach?

I have had the great privilege of training more than 1,300 coaches (at the time of writing in the summer of 2013). That number grows by several hundred every year. Some of them choose to represent our work exclusively and to act as full-time coaches. Many of them choose to integrate the tools they have learned with us into an existing coaching practice. So I have had good opportunities to observe the qualities that make an excellent coach. Here is a quick summary.

Curiosity. A coach is not the same as a teacher. Both have their function in the bigger picture of things, but the difference is this: a teacher has a set of pre-existing ideas, a teaching, that they want to pass on to their students. In some cases the teaching may be inflexible and dogmatic. A coach, on the other hand, comes relatively empty-handed. For sure, a coach has a sophisticated toolbox to draw upon when needed, but their primary function is to be curious about the coachee's reality. *What is your deepest longing? What most gets in the way and obstructs you? What are your greatest triumphs so far in your life? How can I be of service to you?*

In my case, my father was a journalist. Seventy-five percent of what came out of his mouth was questions. Even when I brought friends from school to meet him, he could not restrain himself from firing a barrage of journalistic questions at them. Sometimes, forgetting himself, he even brought out his pen and notebook. He was a questions guy. My father did not have rigid options about what anybody should do—he was just incurably nosy. I think this is partly what has made me a good coach. In my personal life, I pry into other people's business more than I probably should, and often get slapped on the wrist for it by my lovely wife. In a coaching context, this trait is actually welcome. I am curious to know more about my coaching clients, to find out what makes them tick. If you share an incurable curiosity with me, you might make a great coach.

Courage. In my observation a great coach can help a coaching client in areas where the coach themselves has already traversed the challenges as well as the triumphs. If we take writing a book, for example, or a screenplay, or bringing any kind of creative project to completion, the process might look like a piece of cake to the untrained eye. Just sit down at your desk and do it. But the untrained eye has probably never experienced hour after hour of distraction, procrastination, and writer's block. Having written eight books, I know these challenges only too well, and that is what makes me qualified to coach others who want to cross the same terrain. I am not likely to give a writer glib answers such as, "Well, just get up early and put in an hour a day and you'll have it done in no time." That would be frustrating and humiliating. When one of my clients says, "I sit for hours staring at the screen, and nothing comes," I can say, "I know exactly how you feel. I've been through it so many times myself. Let's do some Radical Releasing and try some Empowerment Practices for things you've not yet brought to the situation."

Now let's turn up the courage dial a few notches and meet Ursula Kauer, a Certified Awakening Coach from Stuttgart, Germany. For most of her adult life, Ursula has dealt with issues around her body. She has experienced compulsive eating, tried diets that did not work for long, and often known thoughts that tell her she is not beautiful as she is. Ursula has passed through all this with tremendous courage and determination over many years. It is not that she has slimmed down to become a bathing-suit model suddenly, but the judgments she has held about herself have definitely slimmed down tremendously, while at the same time her acceptance of her body, just as it is, has grown and expanded.

Recently, Ursula was teaching at a training for coaches near Frankfurt. She was scheduled to give a talk that night to the students. As we broke for dinner she stood up and announced in a loud voice, "I want to remind you all to come to my talk tonight. You're going to love it. One of the best things about listening to me speak is that when I laugh, every part of my body shakes." I felt such respect for Ursula in that moment, such pride, to see the way she embodies everything we work on together. She has come into a deep acceptance of herself, and she is ready to give her gifts enthusiastically, using this body as a vehicle. Ursula had to pass through many difficult experiences and face the frequencies in herself that she had resisted her whole life. This required indescribable courage in staying present with things as they are. It is exactly this courage that makes her the best qualified person I know to help other people, particularly women, to make peace with their bodies.

Recreate yourself. Many centuries ago, the poet Bunan wrote:

> *Die while alive,*
> *And be absolutely dead.*
> *Then do whatever you want;*
> *It's all good.*

Bunan is not talking about a physical death, or causing any harm to the body. He is talking about a willingness to let go constantly of the definitions you have placed upon yourself, so that you can become more of a mystery than a person, both to yourself and to everybody else. The most mature answer I know to the question "Who are you?" is "I don't know." In our particular school, when coaches train to be certified, we ask them to give and receive Radical Releasing every day for ninety consecutive days. During their training the coaches keep digging deeper into more and more layers of resisted and forgotten points of view. This willingness to let go constantly of who you thought you were, and to relax into being an undefined mystery, allows you to show up, not as a wave called Joe Blow with his stories and limitations, but as the whole ocean, as all of humanity.

It is this rigorous discipline of letting go of false layers of identity that allows you to have genuine, rather than fabricated, compassion for your coaching clients.

Open to feedback. Coaching is a very young profession. As we have already discussed, a little more than twenty years ago it existed only in the realm of sports. It is a profession that is continually re-inventing itself, and hence every good coach is every day in a process of learning. As a coach it is a really good idea to ask your clients for feedback frequently: How well am I serving you? How could this process go even better for you? What have we left unexplored? In many professions you would never dream of doing this: there is too much at stake, too much of a sense of "I'm a professional, I know what I'm doing; stand aside please, I have the situation under control." Of course, in some professions it would not be advisable. I really would not want a surgeon waking me up in the middle of the operation to ask me if he could do his job better. But coaching is a collaborative relationship, and a willingness to learn the capacity to be undefended is a very important quality for a great coach.

Love. OK, finally it's time to roll out the big L word. Someone told me it has been trademarked by Hallmark Greeting Cards, but I am going to take a risk and use it here anyway.

When my children were young, I wanted to find a really visionary school where they could grow and prosper. I went to visit our local charter school, which had been founded along the principles laid down by Rudolf Steiner, founder of Waldorf education. I have written about this experience more extensively in my book *The Translucent Revolution*.[28] The first time I went to the school, before my children were enrolled, I could not restrain myself from crying, I was so touched by what I saw in the classrooms. What was it exactly? I remember the seventh-grade teacher sitting—not at his desk but on his desk—leading a conversation with his class about democracy. These were twelve and thirteen year olds, but the teacher had such a palpable respect for and curiosity about their opinions. I could feel that he understood evolution and he had no argument with the fact that these small human beings in front of him, having been born in at a later

---

[28] http://better-than-sex.kajabi.com/posts/waldorf-education

time in history, were more evolved than he was. He was using the educational process to draw out the children's wisdom.

Great schoolteachers don't develop such an attitude overnight. Rudolf Steiner used to ask his teachers, at the original Waldorf school, created for the employees of the Waldorf-Astoria cigarette factory in Stuttgart, to perform a little visualization each night. He asked the teachers to think of each child for a few moments before going to sleep. He asked them to reflect upon the highest possibility of that child: the greatest they could accomplish; the peak of love and creativity, happiness and service they could contribute. This is certainly not part of the job description for teachers in the average K-12 school in the United States; but when teachers are willing to do it, it helps to make them truly great. I call that kind of attention, that kind of truly wishing the best for someone and seeing their truest potential, by a specific word. I call it Love. People use that word in all kinds of ways, but that is what I mean by Love. That's my story and I'm sticking to it.

A great coach loves their coaching clients. A great coach will spend a sacred part of each day evoking each client in awareness and feeling into and visualizing their deepest potential, their unique gift, their highest expression of their true nature.

I'm sure there are lots of other qualities that make a great coach, and when checking out different schools it would be good to ask them what qualities they value in their coaches.

I will not go into detail about our own approach here. We have several classes that we offer both online and residential, and we have our own certification process. You can find all the details at awakeningcoachingtraining.com.

Wow, just look at the time. It flies by when you are talking about what you most love. So many people came to the party today with questions about Awakening Coaching, and I promised to answer some of them. Looks like everyone has gathered already in the living room. Let's join them there.

Your Questions Answered

CHAPTER 16

Masculine and Feminine Practice

Is this coaching the same for men and women?

It is a great question. I know that you have heard me talk already about awakening, and Empowerment Practices that can help us to live awakening in day-to-day life. We think we know a lot about these topics already, from traditions that go back thousands of years. But really we only know the masculine expression of these things.

About twelve years ago, I met a woman who had a natural affinity for conscious feminine practice. She was a deep practitioner, and she had come to recognize that she had been over-influenced by masculine traditions. She had a commitment to discovering practices that were suited to bringing forth a feminine embodiment of awakening. Once I got to know her, I was so enamored that I asked her to marry me. Please let me introduce you to my wife, Chameli Ardagh. She can tell you better than I can what feminine practice means:

> *Feminine practice is in the body. It is embodied. It is an exploration of embodied spirituality. It is an exploring of spirit and a relationship to spirit as form, as it appears as form. It embraces our humanity. It embraces all of our challenges and glories of our humanness. It is not a journey, or a reaching away from all of this. It is a deep dive into the body, into feelings, into form, into relationship. And through that, touching and confronting the essence, or the inside of the inside, of experience.*

Many women experience relief and a sense of homecoming when they discover what we can call the feminine practices; because what they have learned to associate with spirituality often feels very restrictive for a woman. A lot of traditions teach us that we need to overcome our feelings. Family and relationships, which are often very central in a woman's life, are looked upon as distractions to spiritual awakening or maturity. Our models of spiritual maturity do not look like most women, or behave like most women. It is a constant comparison and falling short, which has been a crime against women for so long.

In the meeting of feminine spirituality, there is a tremendous freedom to be mirrored by other women and by female archetypes of spiritual maturity, where we discover that spiritual maturity has as many faces as the stars in the sky. It is so rich and multifaceted. It gives women this kind of opportunity and assignment of not trying to fit into a ready-made mold, but to tap into how spirit takes form so radically fresh and spontaneously through each one of us.

The Most Fundamental Distinction

That which is revealed to anyone in a moment of true awakening is always the same. It is limitless consciousness, with no color, or texture, or shape; with no sound to it, with no past or future. It is empty of content, but absolutely full of love, full of presence. Obviously, that has no nationality, no culture bias, no gender. But as soon as that limitless consciousness begins to be lived, it is expressed through a human form. An Indian or a Texan, a Hindu or a Buddhist, will each express this awakening differently in their lives.

The most fundamental distinction we make between people is their gender. You notice that before anything else. But historically, for thousands of years, almost everything that has been said about these topics has been said by men, for men.

Let's think about it. The religion most of us grew up in was Christianity. And how many disciples did Jesus have? Twelve, right? What was the ratio of men to women? Mohammed, the founder of Islam, was a man, and to this day, all of the imams who teach Islam are men. All of Buddha's first *arahats* were men, and only later did he reluctantly introduce a small order of nuns. We can go on and on. In many Eastern traditions, they go so far as to say that only a man can experience awakening.

One hundred years ago, women had to campaign to get the vote. In the 1970s, women campaigned to be able to participate in the workplace and become judges, and doctors, and lawyers, and politicians. Now there is another wave of evolution happening, of women expressing and actualizing themselves in society. In the early part of the 21st century, women are realizing that they do not need to campaign to participate in a world created by men. We are discovering feminine ecology, feminine leadership, feminine styles of finance or organization. We are also seeing the emergence of a fresh field, called feminine spirituality, and feminine spiritual practice.

Energies not Bodies

Before we go on, I want to make an important distinction in language. The words "male" and "female" describe attributes of a physical body. But I am using the words "masculine" and "feminine" to describe differences in energy. Instinctively, we know the difference. What is masculine energy? If we talk in stereotypes for a moment, what do men like to do on a Saturday afternoon? In most countries they like to watch team sports, such as football, which involve a team of (usually) men trying to get a ball past opponents to a goal at the other end. They try to do this through speed, stealth, and sometimes brute force.

Masculine energy is often focused on achieving goals, on the use of power, on being competitive. But also masculine energy includes being focused, being centered, and being present.

On the other hand, and this is again a gross generalization, for the most part women prefer to watch films about relationships rather than team sports. Sometimes Chameli watches a movie like this. Every now and then I walk through the living room. Somebody is dying; there is some terrible complication in a relationship. It is all very tragic. At the end of the movie, Chameli has gone through half a box of Kleenex; her eyes are red. I say, "My God, that looked like it was awful." Between the sobs she replies, "No, it was absolutely wonderful. It was so beautiful." She loved the movie because it allowed her to have an unrestricted experience of feeling. That is one of the marks of feminine energy: the capacity to fully feel. The feminine, in all of us, enjoys color and texture and sensation. It is not goal-oriented, but loves to linger in sensations and feelings in the present moment.

Here is the important thing: both men and women have both masculine and feminine energy in some kind of a balance. If you look at this in biochemical terms, on average men have about thirty times more testosterone in their blood than women do. Some have more, some have less. Women do still have some, but much less. On the other hand, they have much more oxytocin and estrogen. One aspect of Awakening Coaching is to recognize and respect the natural balance of masculine and feminine energy for each person and then to support that person to use practices to restore and live that balance.

Unconscious and Conscious Embodiment

There is an additional level of nuance to this conversation. We are talking not only about masculine and feminine energy, but the unconscious and conscious expression of each one.

When a man is run by masculine energy without any conscious presence brought to it, without any element of awakening, he is going to be run by the more unconscious aspects of the masculine. These are the qualities that are generally least attractive to the feminine. Some examples would be destructive competitiveness, being over-analytical and controlling, using force to get what he wants, setting goals in a way that is rigid and unyielding to reality, and being aggressive or violent.

A man can also run masculine energy through his body with some choice and creative gifting. The qualities of the conscious masculine are, generally, what women most love about men. Conscious masculine energy is present, centered, focused on a goal, but in a way that is aware of reality and able to respond and flow. Conscious masculine energy is able to fully feel, but the sense of being present and grounded is always a little stronger than the feeling. Conscious masculine energy shows up fully in each situation, but always with a tinge of humor, because the man has a sense of life being something like a game, in which he participates fully, but without ever getting completely lost. Conscious masculine energy is able to take action, to be decisive, but all the time with the sense of a bigger context in which the game is appearing.

Equally, we could talk about the unconscious and conscious feminine. The unconscious feminine is emotionally dramatic, can be blaming and catty, or addicted to and getting lost in sensory experience. She can be complaining, nagging, and critical.

The conscious feminine, on the other hand, has a body that is open, a heart full of love; and that love is unconditionally forgiving and embracing. She knows how to create harmony and to bring out the best in people and in situations, because of her natural tendency to love and accept. The conscious feminine knows how to feel deeply in any situation, but without getting lost in a story of "why" and "because" and "who did what to whom." She can feel for no reason.

I am fully aware that making these kinds of distinctions between masculine and feminine energy, and their unconscious and conscious expressions, can be deeply offensive to some people, particularly to women who have fought so hard to avoid gender stereotyping. This can seem like a step backwards. The reason we are doing this here is not to enforce gender stereotypes, but to recognize that people become happy when they relax into their natural character. An Awakening Coach needs to be sensitive that they are not imposing gender stereotypes on a client, but simply skillfully feeling into the natural balance of masculine and feminine energy, and allowing that to express itself.

When we use Embodiment Practices in this way, we are really achieving two ends. One is to restore the balance of masculine and feminine energy that is natural for that person. The other is to move from the unconscious to the conscious expression of each energetic type. Obviously, this is a huge topic, and one that can be easily misunderstood. This is the briefest skimming across the top of it.

Practices that Work

Having guided a client into Radical Awakening, into the recognition of that dimension that is completely beyond gender, and having done enough Radical Releasing and given enough Empowerment Practices that the qualities of the natural state start to emanate, a good Awakening Coach will be able to support the client to discover and return to a natural balance of masculine and feminine energy in their conscious expression.

Chameli explains the essence of feminine practices:

> With the emergence of feminine spirituality, we discover new tools and practices to embody that. We have been trained to rely on and live in the mental realm, and it has caused a tremendous imbalance and disembodiment. That disassociation from the body has caused a sense of split and separation: the core of all of our suffering. So the first step

towards embodying feminine spirituality is to get in touch with the body again: to learn to feel the body, to fully inhabit the body, and also to fully experience feelings and sensations in the body.

There is a practice we call "Feel, Kiss, Flow," which is a beautiful way to train or retrain yourself to stay present with a feeling, while the feeling is actually taking place, instead of immediately running to the mental realm.

The first step is to feel. When you have a feeling or experience, feel it, notice it as a sensation in the body. You bring your awareness into the body and you notice it as a sensation. If you are bored, there might be thoughts about wanting to change the situation; but what does boredom feel like in the body? Notice how it feels as a sensation. If you are sad, what does that feel like?

Then you bring your breath to the sensation, as if you are kissing it with your breath from the inside. You breathe towards the sensation, wherever that is, not to make it go away, but to give it more space to be as it is. When the feeling has space, it will flow. Feelings are energy, and energy is always moving and shifting; it cannot stay still. It is the story about the feeling that gets stuck.

That is the practice. Feel, kiss, flow. Feel as a sensation in the body, kiss it with the breath from the inside, giving it space to flow.

Here are some other practices that bring forth conscious feminine energy:

Feel without a story. As Chameli just explained, the essence of conscious feminine energy is the capacity to feel feelings, completely free of thinking. One simple way to do that is to move her body to a variety of different kinds of music. In this practice the coach asks you to write down twelve different feelings that often arise: feelings like anger, sadness, joy, excitement, terror. You then find, from your iTunes music library, one piece of music that expresses each feeling for you. You make these into a playlist. As the music changes from one piece to another, you fully express feeling by moving your body or making sounds. This is great for women to do it with other women. This practice is not dance, in the sense of doing the tango or the waltz or salsa. It allows you to express feelings without any reason for feeling them.

Time with other women. A famous study done at UCLA in the 1990s demonstrated that when women spend time together without an agenda, for example when going out to lunch or shopping together, when they enjoy each other's company and sensuous experience like colors and smells and taste, their levels of oxytocin are dramatically increased. In a woman's body, this is what balances the stress hormones of adrenalin and cortisol. Women return to their natural state of balance when they are able to have time with other women; when they are not talking about work or getting things done.

Sensuous experience. When I have women clients who are forced into masculine roles for their work, I encourage them to use a simple practice when they come home. Take off everything you were wearing for work, even jewelry, and take a shower to wash away the day. You could possibly even follow this by soaking in a bathtub with oils. When you are finished, anoint your body with creams, lotions, or oils, all with good smells. Dress in something flowing and soft, different from work-clothes, and spend the evening with beautiful music, good food, and maybe even candlelight. I have come to discover that just an hour devoted to really indulging these feminine pleasures can be enough to completely balance many hours of running too much masculine energy at work.

Expressions of devotion. The feminine in all of us is naturally inclined towards feeling and expressing adoration and devotion. You could do this by completely loving and adoring your children, or your partner, but you could equally do it by expressing devotion to a statue or a deity. It does not really matter, because it is not the object that is so important as the capacity to feel and express deep, irrational, unconditional devotion through your body.

Here are a few practices also to enhance the conscious masculine. The conscious masculine in all of us is essentially about dropping into the center. Here are some practices to help drop into that center and find balance there.

Qi Gong. One of the best practices for a man to come back to centered masculine energy is the ancient art of Qi Gong, which originated in China with Shao Lin monks five thousand years ago, but is now easily accessible to learn in the West. One of the best Qi Gong teachers who has made this accessible to us is the Master Mantak Chia. Lee Holden, one his students, has made a wonderful series of videos,[29] which you can easily use to integrate these practices into your day. Qi Gong allows a man to very quickly bring his masculine energy back to the center, to be present, and to be able to face the world from a centered place.

Meditation. Thousands of years ago, men and women would perform very different tasks during the day. Men would spend their days hunting. They would be releasing testosterone into their blood throughout the day. When they came home, they would sit silently and stare into the mens' fire, clubs resting by their sides. This act of sitting still and silent, in an erect posture, is the best way to restore testosterone, which for a man means to rid himself of stress and come back to his natural balance. Silent meditation has biochemical reasons why it is ideally suited to cultivate masculine energy. Zazen or Vipassana meditation, for example, can be suited to both men and women, but they are especially good practices to cultivate the masculine.

---

[29] http://leeholden.com/

Time Alone. Just as women relax more deeply into their true nature by being with other women, so a man can come quickly back to his center and presence by being alone. This could be by taking a walk, or going on retreat for a few days. Alone time for a man is one of the best ways for him to find himself again.

Setting and keeping to goals. The masculine in all of us thrives on setting goals, moving towards them, and achieving them, particularly within preset time limits. Our contemporary business world runs like that, because it was created by men. Whenever a man sets up realistic goals for himself and achieves them, he releases dopamine into his brain, allowing him to feel a sense of fulfillment, and to rest in himself.

There are obviously many more practices that our coaches work with to cultivate conscious masculine and feminine energy, but hopefully this will give you a good overview.

CHAPTER 17

Awakening and Enlightenment

Does this process of Awakening Coaching lead to Enlightenment?

Before we can answer this question, we have to have some reference for what this word "Enlightenment" means. It has been used quite freely in English in the last forty years or so, generally to refer to some kind of absolute state of arrival: the final destination in the journey of evolution.

I have had an opportunity to talk to many people over the years about this word, and I can report to you that there is no shared agreement at all about its meaning, or about who would qualify as "Enlightened." Since not everyone agrees about what the word means, or even if it means anything at all, we have to accept that it is a concept to which we can attribute whatever meaning we choose.

The important thing about concepts is not so much whether they are true or false, but what effect they have on our lives. What happens to the quality of your life in this moment if you install the "Enlightenment" plug-in into your belief systems?

People often pin this word on to certain predictable figures, either living or dead. In recent years some of the recipients of this projection have been Maharishi Mahesh Yogi, Bhagwan Rajneesh (Osho), Amrit Desai, Werner Erhard, Baba Muktanada, and many more.

One possible outcome of pinning this word onto another human being is that when they turn out to have some very human characteristics, we feel disappointed and betrayed. There have been many teachers from the Orient in recent years whose followers have put them on a pedestal. Then later it was discovered that the teacher was preaching celibacy but actually having sex with underage girls. Or the teacher was presented as a monk with no possessions, but was actually amassing money in Swiss bank accounts. There have been all sorts of discrepancies like this. The teacher only falls because they were set up above the human condition. You have to put somebody on a pedestal in order for them to fall off. This is one consequence of the "Enlightenment" myth.

We also can also explore what this concept does to the quality of this moment. Generally, when most people speak of "Enlightenment," they speak of a future state, or the state of another person. "Just now, I'm not Enlightened, but in the future, or that person up on that podium there, that is Enlightenment." What does that do to your experience of the present moment? If you hold a concept of a better future, or of somebody who is better than you up on a podium, what does it do to your experience of now? To your capacity to love?

If you make your life about getting to be "Enlightened" later, then your attention is not on what is going on here in your life now. It can easily become another kind of ambition.

Recently, I took a train from Vienna to Munich. It is a spectacularly beautiful ride, through the Austrian countryside. My organizer had bought a second-class ticket for me. Everything was perfectly good. I had a table in front of me. There was a place to recharge in the computer; the dining car was nearby. Everything was fine. Then I went to look for the bathroom. I stepped into the next carriage, and I found myself in First Class. The seats were leather and reclined a little more. "Looks good," I thought. I asked the conductor how much extra I would have to pay to sit here. 40 Euros more. Not bad. Then I walked a little further down the carriage. I found a private compartment. This was not just First Class, it was VIP Business Class. You get your own little light; the seat reclines all the way back. "Fantastic! I have to sit here."

Life is always like that: there is always an upgrade. You can upgrade your seat, you can upgrade the RAM in your computer, you can upgrade your car, your house, your job. You can even upgrade your husband or your wife. In fact, for most of us, our entire life is about upgrades. These are the symptoms of the generic discontent we suffer from in Western countries: always wanting more, and different, and better.

As I was standing in the Business Class compartment of this Austrian train, thinking how fantastic this could be for me, I stopped. "Arjuna," I said to myself. "It is perfectly fine where you already are. It will make no difference to your enjoyment of the ride to sit here. The views of the mountains are already stunning." I went back to my seat in Second Class and thoroughly enjoyed my train journey.

Enlightenment is the ultimate neurosis of upgrade. You can drive yourself crazy, thinking "There is something wrong with me as I am. I'm having thoughts. Oh, my God, now I'm having negative thoughts. Now I'm thinking about ice cream. I'm having feelings in my body. I'm having feelings down here, in my groin. I need to become Enlightened."

The possibility is not that you fulfill the fantasy of the upgrade, but that you go back to your seat and enjoy the ride of your human life. We are not talking here about an idea of Enlightenment, or about becoming better in any way. Awakening is different from that. It means to really see things as they already are. Not to upgrade, but to recognize that this moment is already perfect. What can you see just now? What can you hear? Who is close to you? Who could you reach out and touch or kiss? There are so many blessings, so easily overlooked in the stampede for more, and different, and better.

This moment is already perfect as it is; it does not have to change. It is being experienced by consciousness, which also doesn't have to change, because it cannot change. It is infinite. For the shift we are talking about, we use the word "awakening." It ends with "I–N–G." A moment of awakening is always now, and now, and now. No brownie points are awarded, no certificate is issued. When we put "E–D" at the end of a word, like "EnlightenED," it becomes about a state; it refers to a moment of graduation, an event in time. "Back in 1991 I became Enlightened." Congratulations. But what about now? This moment is a moment of awakening. Only this moment: all else has been forgotten.

So awakening is not the same as "Enlightenment." It needs no fancy capital letter at the start. It is part of ordinary life. It needs no pedestal. I have done a lot of research on this over the last twenty years. When people fall into awakening in the way that we are describing here, into a recognition of that which is experiencing this moment, the word "Enlightenment" just evaporates; it has no meaning, in either the present or the future. If you ask someone, while they are resting as spaciousness, "Are you enlightened?" they generally just laugh. It doesn't mean anything. If you ask, "Are you trying to become enlightened?" they laugh again.

You might know my 2005 book, *The Translucent Revolution*. I asked everybody I interviewed these same questions: "Are you enlightened? Are you trying to become enlightened?" Out of the 170 people I interviewed, nobody said "yes." They either laughed and said, "I don't even know what that means," or they laughed and said, "No." People were neither claiming it as a present state, nor seeking it as a future state.

People who taste awakening cancel their subscription to this concept. They cancel their subscription to this idea of trying to make this human being perfect. Awakening means not only to drop into a recognition of the awareness that is experiencing this moment, but also to drop into an easygoing acceptance of the way this human animal is, which may be in some ways imperfect. It may have its health issues, it may become forgetful as it gets older, it may be irritable, it may have cravings for things, it has its desires. There might be some interest in training it to behave in an acceptable way, one that is more pleasant to other people; but to try to make this animal perfect is dropped as an unnecessary effort.

CHAPTER 18

Money for Nothing

Many traditions have said that spiritual teachings should be free. Why are you charging for this awakening support?

This is actually something I have thought about a great deal. And it does not have an easy answer. You are absolutely right that in many older cultures—for example, in India, Tibet, or Japan, or here in the West in earlier times—money was often kept separate from anything to do with awakening. The assumption was that commerce would corrupt the teaching. And there is good reason to think that.

In India, for example, a guru would live simply, meditate, pray, and be of service to the local people. He never asked for money. At the same time, however, those people would never go to a teacher empty-handed. They would bring him clothes, food, firewood to keep him warm. There is a word for this in India, *dana*, which means the natural giving back to a teacher. The similar principle of tithing a percentage of your income exists in the church in the West as well. In this way there is an exchange of energy. The teacher could be sustained physically and the local people could be sustained spiritually. Many people have tried this same arrangement in recent decades in Europe and America, but it has not always worked out so well. For the most part, we live in a society where people are used to paying for services.

In recent years we have seen a variety of outcomes to experimenting with different solutions to the money question. One is that well-meaning teachers will offer their services for donation, then find themselves unable to pay their bills. They end up having to put a lot more attention on money than they would like.

181

The second possibility is that a teacher builds up a large organization and charges fees way higher than needed. We have seen teachers from Eastern countries amassing a fleet of Rolls Royces, palaces, and private jets. Something generally feels icky about that to outsiders looking in.

I have come to the conclusion that there is nothing wrong with giving or receiving money: it is the spirit in which it is done, and the use that money is put to, that are more significant.

Creating value

When I was in my mid-thirties, I had an extremely successful school going in Seattle. I was training psychotherapists to integrate hypnosis into their practice. Every course was fully booked, I had enough money to do whatever I wanted, and I accumulated enough in a few years that I could retire and live a simple life.

The longing inside of me for something deeper, something more real, something more nourishing, led to my selling everything. I gave up the school, I sold my house and my car, and I put what little remained into storage. I traveled back to India in search of something I could not name with my mind, but which my heart could not let go of. A year later I met my teacher, H. W. L. Poonja, and he guided me into Radical Awakening. He never asked for money. He lived a modest but comfortable life and had a pension from his work. He also came from a culture where teachers don't ask their students for money. But I had actually paid a huge price to be with him, which caused me to take the whole thing seriously. I had given up my house, my work, the comforts of living in Seattle, in search of something deeper.

What is revealed in a moment of Radical Awakening is incredibly simple. The challenge of that simplicity is not in gaining access to it, but in valuing it. I created value in such a way that awakening became the foundation of my day-to-day life, because of the price I paid, not to my teacher, but to life. In the same way, in our society, people will generally value things when they pay something for them, in one way or another.

How Much Does it Cost?

When I take new clients for a coaching series, one of the first questions they have for me is, "How much does it cost?" I tell them that I do not have a fixed price, but it is a good idea for them to place some value on the process. So, just as we have described earlier, we establish the outcomes that they want to create through coaching. I guide them to think outside of the box, of how this relationship could impact their life in the most meaningful way. Once we have put everything down on paper, and we both know what they want to see as outcomes—whether they are labeled spiritual, physical, financial, or to do with relationship—I ask them this simple question: If you had all these outcomes that you have imagined, what would it be worth to you? What value can you place on that? I think that this is a vital question to ask people, so they can create their own value.

Someone may say, "It is worth tens of thousands of dollars, but I don't have that much." I would never take more money from someone than they felt comfortable with. Even if they can't pay it, they have had an opportunity to create value for themselves. If you are a coach, ask your clients this question. It allows you to create a unique financial relationship with each person. One might pay you many thousands of dollars, because that is what they need to do to create value. Another client may inspire you so much with their vision and their goals, and fill you with compassion so much for the challenges they have passed through, that you are willing to work with them for next to nothing, or even free. I've done both.

Take What You Need and Give Away the Rest.

It is not really money that is the problem here. It is the addiction to *more* that gets us into trouble. It is never-ending. So here is a simple solution to that problem. Figure out what you need in order to pay your rent or your mortgage, food, and travel, and all your other costs for a year. Then tack on a little bit for extras. Add a little more for savings, so you can prepare for your future. Now you know what you need in order for money to no longer be an issue. Once you get clear about what is enough for you, things become very simple. Strangely enough, once you know how much money you need, it comes to you much more easily. Consider giving the rest away. You could do that by donating to charity, or doing some coaching for free.

Instilling the word "enough" in your vocabulary is one of the best ways to overcome confusion around money. Once you know how much you need, and recognize that it is not a big deal to get there, things become simple. Your fear of poverty will evaporate the same day you abandon the endless greed for more.

Offer People Choice

We have a similar arrangement with our Awakening Coaching training. We have priced it quite modestly, relative to other coaching schools. When people fill out the application, we tell them the full price, and we add this statement: "We would love for you to pay this amount if you are able to, as this allows us to cover the expenses of running a course like this. If you really cannot afford this much, we understand. If you need a discount, tell us, and we would be glad to discuss it with you."

Since we have published our prices in this way, things have become very simple. About three-quarters of the people who apply are happy to pay the full amount. About a quarter of the people ask for a discount, and we ask them to briefly explain why they need it. What kind of hardships have they been through? What opportunities will they have to use this coaching in a useful way? This arrangement allows the people who have the money, and who would benefit from paying it, to pay in full. It also gives people who do not have enough money the opportunity still to take the course.

By thinking outside the usual box about money and fees, you can easily find a way for everyone to get what they need, and for money to cease to be an issue.

CHAPTER 19

Who is Qualified?

It sounds like you are training people off the street to become facilitators of awakening. I wonder if they are really qualified for the job.

That is a really good point. The question of who is qualified has dominated this field for thousands of years. Shall we explore some of our traditional assumptions about who should facilitate awakening? It usually involves the idea of somebody being "Enlightened." Historically, and even today, that has been weighted much more towards a masculine figure than a feminine one. In recent years, we have seen the emergence of feminine spiritual figures, but historically it has been slanted towards the masculine.

We are inclined to think that somebody who is qualified is "Enlightened" (with "ED" at the end) and we are not. As we have already discussed, the problem with that way of looking at things is that, although it might have some validity, it can easily become a way of re-enforcing these two roles. The more we spend time with someone who is "Enlightened" or awakened, the more we re-enforce the identity of being a seeker, of not being "Enlightened" or awakened, always waiting for something to happen. Many people get stuck in that role for years or even decades, looking up to a teacher on a pedestal, feeling all the lower for it.

In Awakening Coaching, we emphasize awaken*ing*, and we recognize that there are two important aspects of this. One is having the recognition of your true nature as presence. The other is the embodiment, or the living of that awakening in day-to-day life.

My good friend the brilliant philosopher Ken Wilber has made the important distinction between states and stages. A state, he describes, is a momentary peak experience, where we have a realization way beyond the base level at which we are usually humming. A moment of awakening for most people is a temporary state. We are normally living in a feeling of separation, of striving and effort, and we have a moment of something else. Maybe it is through meditation, or meeting a teacher, sometimes even from taking a drug, where we recognize our nature to be limitless consciousness. That is a temporary state. Moving through stages of evolution means cultivating practices and habits to stabilize those kinds of peak states within the fabric of day-to-day life.

The other important distinction that Wilber makes is that we do not evolve through stages along one line alone. We evolve through stages of development in parenting, in sexuality, in our work, in social and political action, in the way that we take care of our body and our health. There are multiple, parallel lines of development. Almost everybody has an imbalance: far evolved along one line and not so evolved along another. Consequently, the whole idea of somebody being more evolved, or somebody being "Enlightened," really comes into question.

Here is my answer as to who I would say is qualified. First, I would say to be qualified, someone must have a genuinely open heart and mind, and a natural love and care for other people. Whatever their own condition may be, they need to have a natural curiosity and interest in the well-being of other people.

Second, they need to have enough of a realization of their true nature as limitless that they now know, deep down, this is the truth of who they are, and the truth of who the other is, no matter how much they have or have not stabilized that in other areas of their life. Experience has told me that you are a good facilitator of awakening if you know for sure, beyond an intellectual understanding, that who you are is this limitless consciousness.

The third thing I would say is that somebody is qualified to help you in the embodiment of awakening in any area of life where they are familiar with the territory. They have either passed through the journey of mastery in that area, or they are in the process of doing so enough that they know the obstacles and the triumphs.

I remember going to a conference many years ago. Everybody had gathered together to listen to a celibate nun from India, a young woman who had grown up her whole life in her spiritual tradition and almost without doubt had never even been kissed. A very pregnant woman stood up in the audience and said, "I am eight months pregnant, about to have my baby, and I would like to get some guidance from you on how to raise my child." I looked at this scene with disbelief. Why on earth would you ask that question of a celibate nun who has never even contemplated what it would be like to have children? It is crazy! She may be gifted at guiding you in esoteric monastic practices, but one area that she has definitely not even begun to explore is family life.

Very often we do this. We ask for guidance about money from monks or religious figures who never deal with money. We ask for advice about relationship from people who do not have relationships. Someone who is qualified to guide you in the embodiment of awakening in any particular area is someone who has some degree of mastery or experience in that particular area. That is why, when we train coaches, we ask them and encourage them to develop an area or a niche.

For example, Sorel Dietzler, who has been an Awakening Coach for many years, came to Awakening Coaching straight out of a corporate background. She had worked for years as a financial controller within a corporation, and she knew everything there was to know about corporate life. All the hierarchy and stress, climbing the ladder—she was very familiar with it. Now she offers Awakening Coaching to support people, particularly women, to make the shift out of the corporate environment towards doing what they would truly love to do with their precious human life.

She is extremely qualified to talk about that subject because she knows awakening enough that she can speak from Inspired Certainty, and she also knows the corporate world enough to guide you through the potholes and the ravines that you encounter unexpectedly.

CHAPTER 20

Awakening Coaching and Psychotherapy

How is the work you do with people different from psychotherapy?

That is also an excellent question, and important to understand. Here is one way I can explain it to you. Imagine that while I'm asleep I have a dream in which someone is really angry with me. In the dream, I try to protect myself from the anger. I try to improve my self-esteem and my communication skills, so I can handle the situation. I seek support to get the angry person out of my life. I sit down with the angry person and ask, "What did I do to hurt your feelings? How can I make it better?" Still in the dream, I meet a psychotherapist. We flash back to times when my mother or father were angry with me, and I understand that the angry person is somehow connected to those times. Then I wake up in the morning. Where did the angry person go? Poof! Gone. The problem of having someone angry with me was not solved and did not even need to be analyzed. It dissolved because I was just having a dream. I woke up and recognized the problem as an illusion.

If you have a strong interest in the story of your life, why it is the way it is, how it got to be this way, and what you need to do to change it, then often the skills of a psychotherapist will be better suited to you than Awakening Coaching. If you had a difficult childhood, and the relationship with one of your parents still presses heavily on you today, just snapping your fingers and waking up from your dream may not work. It may be necessary to fully feel the feelings, and to stay in the story long enough that it resolves.

190

There comes a point for many people, however, when they get tired of their own story. It is like a soap opera, where after the ninth season, and the 157th episode, you just say, "Enough! I don't think I want to watch this show anymore." When that becomes true for you, than an approach like Awakening Coaching might be more suitable.

When Coaching Is Not the Right Choice

There is another aspect to this as well. There are times when Awakening Coaching might be ill-advised and somebody absolutely needs the services of a psychotherapist or psychiatrist. When you go the gym, you may decide to work with a trainer. The trainer can show you how to use the equipment and how many reps to do on each machine, then set you up with a program that will lead to better health. However, if you have a serious injury—for example, a dislocated shoulder or a torn ligament in your knee—you would be ill-advised to go straight to a gym and engage the services of a trainer without informing them of the injury. You could, in fact, hurt yourself more. If you have a physical injury, you are better off going to a doctor or a surgeon, or some kind of licensed health-care professional who knows how to help you to heal. Sure, once you are fully healed, you could go back to the gym and talk to the trainer.

When someone has a physical injury, it is clear to everybody that it is a real limitation that needs remedial action. But we are not always so understanding about mental and emotional suffering. Depression, for example, or anxiety or compulsive behavior are real conditions, just like a torn ligament. They need to be treated by professionals who have been trained to address these problems.

A Hybrid Approach

There are times when you can use both approaches simultaneously. I have had several coaching clients over the years who were suffering from mental or emotional illness. They were under the care of a psychiatrist, who had prescribed medication. But they also felt inspired to add awakening to the mix. In a situation like that, an Awakening Coach can develop a cooperative relationship with the health-care professional. I ask the psychiatrist for written permission to work with their client, and we talk on the phone. In this way we can work side by side. I can help the patient to relax more deeply into their true nature, into infinite consciousness without limits. And I can help them to use Radical Releasing to free resistance. The psychiatrist is also there to help the client deal with deep-seated issues and trauma, which they are skilled at treating. In every case I have done this, the psychiatrist reported much faster results from the therapy, and frequently the client was able to get off medication more quickly. The more expanded view of awakening provided fertile soil for the psyche to heal. In fact, often it is only possible to make significant adjustments to the mechanism of the psyche when you have enough space around it to realize you are not the psyche.

Your computer has an operating system written to the hard drive. That is what the computer "boots up" from. If there is something wrong with the operating system, you cannot start the computer from there. You have to start it up from something else, then make changes to the operating system. In the same way, if you are completely identified with your thoughts and beliefs and you think that is who you are, it is relatively difficult to make adjustments to the story, because a broken operating system is running you in that moment. If you have enough space around the psyche to recognize that you are this spacious consciousness, you are this which was never born and can never die, then you can see the bundle of thoughts and beliefs as more of a computer program. That allows you to make changes to the program, because you are looking at it from a different perspective.

When Is Awakening the Right Choice?

Awakening Coaching is the right choice for you when you have run through your story enough times that it has become boring. You may not have resolved everything, and as a matter of fact that is highly unlikely to be true. But the endless effort to try and fix yourself has become exhausting.

For example, remember Karen Fritz who we met earlier at the party? She had suffered postpartum depression after the birth of her second child, and went through years of trying to deal with that. She came to Awakening Coaching, not because she had resolved her depression, but because she reached the point of realizing it was something she needed to be with, and deal with, rather than get rid of. She tried pharmaceuticals, she tried different kinds of therapy, both of which contributed in their own way, but they had not made the problem go away. When she integrated awakening into her view, it did not make the problem go away either. On the contrary, it allowed her to relax more deeply into the depression and receive the lessons and teachings it had to offer her. It became an ally. It became a means for deepening into herself rather than an obstacle. That is what happens when we integrate awakening into our lives: we do not solve our problems, we dissolve them. They cease to be problems when they are seen from a larger perspective. They become the journey itself instead of an obstacle to the journey.

Let me summarize a few key differences between a classical psychotherapeutic or psychiatric approach and Awakening Coaching.

The Client. We have already mentioned that the kind of client who comes for psychotherapy is generally someone who is identified with their story and wants to heal or resolve it. They want to fix themselves. In contrast, the kind of client who comes for Awakening Coaching has tried that enough to become bored with their story and they want to wake up from the story rather than fix it.

The intention of psychotherapy is to bring healing or resolution at a personal level. The intention of Awakening Coaching is to shift the attention from being fixated on the personal level to something broader and more expansive.

Perceived Obstacles. What is perceived as an obstacle is different in each case. Many times, somebody going to psychotherapy will see that their childhood or their beliefs and habits are an obstacle to a good life. In Awakening Coaching we recognize that only the identification with those things, or the resistance to those things, is the obstacle. When anything is fully experienced, it becomes a gateway.

Relationship. The way these two approaches view intimate relationship is very different. Most kinds of psychotherapy focus on behavioral change to produce a more harmonious or respectful outcome between two people. Awakening Coaching focuses on dissolving the sense of separation between two people, so that it can open a portal where you see yourself as both distinct from the other and one with the other at the same time.

The Past. The way the two approaches view the past and childhood is also different. Psychotherapy sees your past as real, and the cause of your suffering as needing to be resolved. This often involves doing regression. Awakening Coaching focuses on stabilizing the realization that the past is not real now: it is just a thought in this moment.

Desire. Many kinds of psychotherapy and coaching recognize that to be happy we need to be clear what we want to get out of life and find ways to fulfill our desires. Awakening Coaching helps you to see the limited nature of those desires and to relax into a deeper sense of longing and coming home to yourself.

Self-Esteem. Most kinds of psychotherapy would recognize low self-esteem as an obstacle, and would aim to build self-esteem, so you feel more confident about yourself. Awakening Coaching recognizes, in a humorous way, that any level of self-esteem is too much. Having esteem for a separate entity is an illusion, and where the esteem really needs to be pointed to is not a separate entity called "me" but the mysterious source of life that flows through everything.

Self-Love. The final distinction is the idea of self-love. A lot of types of psychotherapy encourage you to love yourself more. In Awakening Coaching we recognize there is no "you" to be loved, and so love becomes a function of consciousness seeing beauty in the world. We abandon the idea of loving yourself and relax into being something more spacious. Then love is what happens when that spaciousness perceives itself dancing as form in the world.

CHAPTER 21

Deeper Love Coaching

What kind of impact does Awakening Coaching have on intimate relationships?

I love it that you are asking this question. Many people come to talks or seminars that I give who have spiritual aspirations. "I want to make the ego disappear." "I want to be permanently established in limitless consciousness." All of that is just fine, and we can either fulfill the longings or cause them to dissolve, to relax. Less often someone will say to me, "I have a longing to love deeply." It gets me every time. The person who asks could be single or in a relationship—it makes no difference. To my ears, the longing to open your heart fully to another human being, to love deeply and in an undefended way, is the sweetest, most innocent, and most vulnerable longing we can find within ourselves.

When anyone brings awakening consciousness to impact their intimate life, it allows for a very different experience of relationship. Broadly speaking, there are three possible relationships that anyone can have to intimacy. Let's examine them briefly.

Dependent, Anti-Dependent, and Beyond

The first relationship is one we are all familiar with, and we can label it "dependent." This means you have the feeling you are missing something within yourself, and the compulsive sense that if you can just find the right person to give you what you need, you will feel whole and complete.

I feel sure you know what happens if you go to a party with this feeling of needing somebody, looking for somebody to make you whole and complete. It is hardly an effective dating strategy. If you do eventually meet someone from this place of need, it is likely to be someone with a similar sense of need. If the two of you can manage to align your projections, you may be able to convince yourselves, and each other, that you each have the magic key to "make" your partner happy. What follows is the ultimate joy-ride, the biggest rush of endorphins available on planet Earth at this time. Until you crash, that is. We call it "falling" in love for good reason.

This kind of relationship, based on projection, need, and feeling incomplete, is commonly referred to as "codependency." It is the kind of relationship where you are willing to compromise and twist yourself into distorted shapes in order to appear indispensable to the other person and guarantee they are never going to leave you. The other person will do the same thing, until the pressure builds sufficiently that one of you feels compelled to bust free. Then the game is over.

The second kind of relationship we can develop to intimacy is the polar opposite. You have been hurt enough times, you have been burned enough times, you have been rejected enough times, that you make the decision you are never going to expose yourself again. You draw a line in the sand. "I don't need anything from anybody. Nobody can give me what I want. I have everything within myself. I can find the inner masculine and the inner feminine. I can experience union and love within myself. I don't need to get any of this from the outside." If you meet another person from that place, once more you will almost certainly attract a partner who is your mirror. When two people meet who are convinced they do not need anything from anybody else, it creates a relationship we can call "anti-dependent." You meet occasionally on weekends. Maybe you go out to dinner once or twice a week, always splitting the bill down the middle. You might even have other lovers and call it an "open" relationship. There are no ties, no commitment; everyone is left free to do what they want. You manage to stay free of getting entangled, but you might also discover, sooner or later, that you are missing something, too. You never find out what it is like to go really deep, to experience real intimacy. Deep down, you may feel separate and lonely.

The third possible relationship to intimacy requires more insight, more practice, and more maturity. We call it the Deeper Love. This is where you drop deeply enough into awakening, into that dimension of yourself which is free, which has no boundaries, which needs nothing from anybody, and you rest there long enough, marinate in it and as it, that it starts to warm up. Then it naturally wants to give itself as a gift.

Many of us have already experienced this in becoming a parent or looking after a small child. With a small child, there is no mutual exchange. You do not make the deal "I'll take care of you, if you take care of me. I'll wash your diapers, if you take out the garbage." When you are in relationship with a small child, it is all about giving. In a practical and material sense you just give and give and give, and that proves amazingly fulfilling. The child is not doing anything for you in return. The child is just there, looking at you with wide-open eyes. Many people say this is the time when they felt the most love in their life.

Similarly, it is possible, through practice, to relax deeply enough into that dimension of yourself which is free. You gradually recognize and release the protective mechanisms that have kept you feeling separate in relationship. Then you can enter into a radically new relationship to intimacy, based in overflow, generosity, and giving. It certainly changes the way you have sex. You are no longer entering into sex to gain pleasure or release for yourself. You are giving the gift of love to your partner through your body.

Who Is Looking for the Deeper Love?

In Awakening Coaching, the clients who come to us because they want to deepen intimacy fall into two categories. One is people who are single and are looking for the next relationship to go deeper and be more fulfilling than anything in the past. The other is people who are already in relationships and want to experience greater intimacy with their partners.

It is easier to deepen the relationship of single people to intimacy. When you don't have a fixed person in your life who is used to you showing up in a certain way, you can change your habits quickly. In a matter of weeks you can shift from being stuck in dependency or anti-dependency to the Deeper Love. The art is to cultivate, through tastes of awakening to spaciousness, the habit of overflow, of generosity, of giving. We have many different tools that we use in coaching to make this habit stronger.

When we work with couples, there are all sorts of practices they can do together to move into an overflow of fullness—far more than we can cover here. Some of the basic ones are: expressing appreciation, giving presence through the body or through the eyes, and sexual practices that allow a shift from a sexuality based in release to one based in giving and circulating energy.

Let's examine the basic principles of all our practices now, to give you a sense of what it is like to bring conscious practice to relationship.

Deeper Love Practice

Honesty. Telling the truth about your experience in this moment is not just a moral virtue; it is a practice that brings more awakening to relating. The kinds of practices we use involving honesty are not so much about stories from the past as about now. Connecting your immediate experience of this moment to the words coming out of your mouth dissolves separation and the sense that someone is in control outside of the experience itself. Try a relationship practice like this here.[30]

Pure Listening. We can listen to fix, to understand, to analyze, to criticize, or to sympathize. Pure listening, in contrast, means to listen like the sky. Have you ever noticed that when you shout up into the open sky, it is simply present? It never interrupts, or offers advice, or judges you. It never puts its fingers in its ears. This is one of the most deepening, healing, nourishing qualities to bring to intimate relationship: the possibility of bringing all of you to this moment, listening without reactivity.

Learning to listen in its purity has a powerful effect on both the one listening and the one being listened to. Try a listening practice here.[31]

Feel Without a Story. We have already talked about this principle when we looked at feminine practices. It is the essence of setting the feminine heart free of the shackles of "why" and "because" and the requirement for feeling to be reasonable. There are many ways to tell your partner what you are feeling, and to stay free of blame or logic. Try a practice like this here.[32]

Humor. Perhaps you may remember, when we talked about Empowerment Practices, that I told you about Luigi. Chameli and I created Luigi to bring more humor and creativity to the unconscious habit of jealousy. We have found the same thing many times in working with couples and singles: we cannot always change the habits themselves; but when we turn them into humor and art, they become a way of giving more love, sharing more of yourself, rather than obstacles to love. Try a practice like this here.[33]

---

[30] http://better-than-sex.kajabi.com/posts/here-nowing--2
[31] http://better-than-sex.kajabi.com/posts/pure-listening
[32] http://better-than-sex.kajabi.com/posts/feel-without-a-story
[33] http://better-than-sex.kajabi.com/posts/humor-practices

Commitment. Living in the flow of the Deeper Love is about remembering why you want to be in a relationship in the first place, restoring your priorities, and then living from that place. Once you know why you are here, and you are committed to that, the relationship becomes simple. With Deeper Love Coaching, we do not encourage people to think about being committed to a person or a situation. That is secondary. The commitment is to love itself, to living awakening in every aspect of your life.

Chameli and I, for example, as well as all the couples we have worked with, live monogamously. We are both fiercely committed to living our deepest realization in every moment, to living honestly and openly, to squeezing every drop of juice from each moment of life. That is the commitment we reaffirm every day, to ourselves and to each other. We stand side by side in our commitment, encouraging each other, reminding each other, calling on each other when we forget. We have found that a monogamous relationship with the right partner is the most effective way to keep that kind of commitment. Try a practice about commitment here.[34]

Appreciation and Worship. The most important practice we can bring to relationship is the conscious practice of worship. When we have done interviews about this, people often wonder if they heard the question right. "'Worship?' Surely you meant to say 'respect' or 'friendship'?" "No," we reply, "You heard us right. We practice worship in intimate relationship. Yes, like a religious ritual."

We may not always feel like worship: that is why it needs practice. It is so easy to put endless energy in relationships into what is wrong, what needs fixing or processing or forgiving or working on. We tend to overlook the indescribable mystery and blessing that here is a living being in front of us, who has opened up deeply enough that we can see below the surface into the deeper currents.

---

[34] http://better-than-sex.kajabi.com/posts/commitment--10

The practice of worship requires us to look beyond the personality, the likes and dislikes and beliefs that populate the shallow waters of a person, and to seek out the vast forces, the ones that hover between personal and universal. If you look deeply enough into your partner, whatever story he or she may carry, you will find endless depth, and you will fall to your knees in awe. Try a practice to open the current of worship here.[35]

---

[35] http://better-than-sex.kajabi.com/posts/couples-puja--3

CHAPTER 22

Anticipate Resistance

I tried getting coached before, but it didn't really work. There was a limit to where I could go. Why would Awakening Coaching be any different?

Coaching is a collaborative relationship between the coach and the client. They enter into an agreement, from the very beginning, that they are going to support each other in creating certain outcomes. From the outset, it is clear that the client has not been able to make those changes on their own. Whether it is to drop more deeply into awakening, to show up differently in relationship, or to improve their health and their diet, the client has been unable to do it alone, and they have engaged a coach for support.

Let us take a simple example. The client knows that if they eat well, and drink plenty of water, they have more energy and feel better, or if they meditate each day, their day goes more smoothly. If they relax back into being spacious consciousness, a lot of problems clear up on their own. It is obvious that the client wants this outcome. But it is also obvious that there is some level of self-sabotage, or they would be doing these things already.

Dimensions of You

There is a simple explanation as to why we encounter such enormous resistance to the very things that we think we most want. The answer is to be found in a deeper examination of who or what we really are.

One level of who you are, which we have already explored plenty together, is limitless consciousness. You are unborn, undying natural awareness, which has no preference for anything, no craving or desire for anything, but also has no resistance to anything. This spacious consciousness is present with what is.

In another dimension, you are a body. Frequently, when you say, "I'm going to the store" or "I have a stomachache," what you are referring to is a body. The body is a kind of animal. Just as with other animals, the body does not experience a lot of internal conflict. It has natural, innocent desires: it wants to eat when it is hungry, sleep when it is tired. Just like any animal, or a small baby, it has its desires, and when they are satisfied, it is content for a while.

In the middle, between natural awareness which has no preferences and the body which has very simple, conflict-free desires, there is a gray zone. This is where the trouble starts. We often assume that the gray zone is a single thing. We refer to it as "the mind," or as "the ego," or even sometimes as "me." The me says "my body" and "my awareness." Whatever it is, it is not clearly defined. It is actually the very vagueness of that middle ground, this gray zone between the body and awareness, that gets us into trouble.

Document Your Thoughts

Here is the key to understanding resistance, which makes it quite simple. Start paying attention to what is going on in the gray zone. Take note of the thoughts and reactive feelings, which frequently repeat themselves. They change very quickly, so you will have to pay close attention. It is like trying to watch a mosquito moving around the room: it darts around and changes position quickly. One of the benefits of meditation is that it is a way to pay attention to what is going on in that gray zone—what is going on with thoughts and feelings.

Let me share with you one of the practices we frequently give to our coaching clients. Each day, write down five thoughts that seem familiar visitors: they occur frequently. For example, "I'm not good enough," or "There's not enough time," or "I can't afford it," or "I don't deserve it." Write them down: get them on paper. Do this every day for a week or two. Fairly quickly you will discover that the mind, or the ego, or whatever we want to call this gray zone, is not really one thing at all. It would be better to say that it is a collection, a crowd of multiple voices and personalities, which are frequently in conflict with one another. Certainly, there is a part of you, a voice, that is really motivated to get up early, exercise, and eat healthful food. But there is another voice, another part, that will go to great lengths to make sure none of that happens. And so we progress along our intended journeys in fits and starts: sometimes elated, frequently discouraged and ashamed.

That is exactly why you may need a coach or to get support. If there was just one of you, things would be very simple. Decide to exercise every day, and lo and behold, that is what happens. Recognize just one time that you are limitless consciousness, beyond birth and death, and all fear disappears instantly—life becomes a play. But you are not one coherent entity, as a little research will demonstrate, so a coach can support you to recognize, and even anticipate, resistance and then to work with it.

Another way to understand the activity in the gray zone is that these thoughts are not exactly yours at all, anyway. They do not really belong to a separate person called "me." If you write down the thoughts and reactive feelings and start to catalogue them, you will discover that many of them bear a striking resemblance to the thoughts and operating beliefs of your parents and grandparents, and to the popular thoughts and beliefs of your culture, your religion, or your peer group. All of these repeating beliefs are borrowed from a variety of sources. They are imitative. And they are in conflict with each other.

As these voices become more apparent to you, your coach can do Radical Releasing with you to take off the resistance from each one. When we do Radical Releasing on a resisted point of view, it tends to relax. As a result, action becomes smoother and more effortless, while at the same time you rest more deeply in your natural state of awareness.

There are many of ways to work with this. Once you recognize that certain beliefs are bubbling up again and again, you discover that within you there seems to be a lost child, a control freak, a homeless person, a ruthless army officer, and a crowd of others. You discover an endless array of these voices, or "sub-personalities."

It takes considerable discipline and the support of a good coach to become aware of them and realize that they are in conflict; but once we do, two things become possible that have a huge impact on resistance and sabotage.

The Adult Self

The more you develop awareness of these conflicting parts or voices, the more you can strengthen and cultivate a neutral adult observer. This is not just limitless pure consciousness, which only observes. It is also a voice, also a part. The difference is that it is aware of all the other voices. It can make decisions, it can participate in life, but it does not have a charge, or an agenda, in the same way the other voices do. The more you observe the other parts and do nothing, the more the qualities of that neutral observer come to the surface.

Imagine that the gray zone is like a minivan, full of these parts that are calling out for their needs. "I want to stop for ice cream," shouts one. "I want to go back to where we came from," says another. "Go faster, go faster, go faster!" shouts another. "I am scared, we're going to crash—slow down," cries another. "I want pizza." "Follow that sports car." "Exit here!" "I need to get home NOW! I'm missing my TV show!" The Adult Self is like the driver. It hears all of the demands, takes them all into consideration, and then decides where to go based on what is best for everyone, including the other drivers and minivans around.

The Adult Self does what is required. It is not so fixated on "I want, I need." It is aware of the spectrum of needs for the whole environment and it does what is needed. Many of us discover this Adult voice when we become parents. If your child wakes up in the middle of the night with a fever, you don't get obsessed at that point with questions of "What do I need? I need my sleep. I don't want to get up. Oh, maybe I should. Well, let me think about this...." You just get up and deal with it. For many of us, parenting is such a powerful evolutionary practice because it gets us out of our obsession with ourselves and brings us back to an awareness of what is needed outside of our own personal, selfish needs. As we cultivate the Adult Self, becoming more aware of what is needed, there is more space for the unique gift to emerge and to be given.

Enter a Dialogue

Another outcome is that it becomes possible to listen to, and even dialogue with, these different voices. Maybe you have a task to complete. I often work with creative people who are writing a book or a screenplay, trying to get a project completed that they feel is of service. Some voice within them feels an obligation, realizes there is a deadline, wants to make a contribution and get it finished. Then there is another voice that says, "I don't want to do this. I want to go to the beach. I want to go out for breakfast. I want to watch TV."

Now, we recognize there are some parts or voices that are ambitious, which have a sense of responsibility and loyalty, and another part or voice which is like a teenager and just wants to rebel. We can talk to that rebellious part. We can become curious and find out, "What do you need? What are you afraid of? What would it take for you to feel satisfied and relax?"

You can try this today, using two cushions or two chairs. Start by sitting on one of the cushions, and imagine or visualize this disconnected part on the other cushion. It might be a small child of five years old, or a teenager wearing gothic clothes, or anything else you can imagine.

Talk to this part like this: "I am here for you. I know that I have not always paid enough attention to you, and that you have felt you needed to act up to get attention. I am here now. I want to listen to you and understand you."

After a minute or so, stop speaking, and just listen to what this part has to say to you. At first the part may appear to be quite sullen, and not want to talk at all. Or it may just mutter something like, "Why should I trust you now? You have always let me down before."

After another minute of listening, talk to this part again. Be patient, be curious.

Now you can stand up, shift your body over and become this other part. Sit on the other cushion. Use your body to adopt the posture of this part. If it is a lost child, then hug your knees to your chest, and rock to and fro a little. Talk as this part.

You can go back and forth several times in this way, from the Adult Self to the isolated part, for no more than ten minutes. Remember to always finish the practice on the Adult cushion. Otherwise you may spend the rest of your day as a rebellious teenager! Finish by picking up the other cushion, hold it to you, reassure this fragmented part that you will be back tomorrow, take a breath, and integrate this part back into wholeness.

If you do this kind of dialogue over several days, the relationship will shift and evolve. The child becomes happier and less needy. The teenager feels less isolated. Once you recognize the needs of this part, it is easy to make deals that will allow the part to relax and to cooperate with the needs of the whole. "OK, so now I understand that you need more play time. And I know that you have not had that much lately. So if we write now for a couple of hours, and then we go bounce on the trampoline, go for a walk, or play with the dog outside, will that work for you?"

It is not necessary to keep doing this for very long. Once a part is recognized and heard, once its needs are addressed, it gets integrated back and ceases to give trouble. As a result, the resistance becomes less, and the Adult Self becomes more developed.

By becoming aware of the conflict within the psyche, by strengthening the observer but also taking care of the needs of these different parts, you discover that the conflict becomes less, and that you are able to do the things you need to do more effectively.

It Is Life that Works

So, to come back to your question, we do not need to be so concerned about whether Awakening Coaching works or not. It is a tool—a collection of tools, in fact. If they are used effectively, we get the outcomes we are looking for.

The great liberation is not to find a method that works, but to discover that you fundamentally work, life fundamentally works, when you wake up to what is real and what is imaginary. Once we clearly see the fragmented nature of the psyche, once we become familiar with the internal conflict between different voices, then we can work with it. Then we discover not that one particular method works, but that everything works when we anticipate and handle resistance.

Tell me your thoughts about this.

CHAPTER 23

Endless Distraction

What most gets in the way of this style of coaching being effective?

I remember one day in India when several of us were gathered with our teacher, H. W. L. Poonja. He liked to tease us.

"What is the one thing that most gets in the way of freedom?" he asked.

"The mind," somebody suggested. "The ego," said another. He shook his head dismissively. "Concepts," said somebody else. "Beliefs." This game went on for maybe half an hour. Finally, he gave us the answer he was looking for.

"Distraction," he said. "Distraction: that is the only thing that stands between you and freedom." And then he told us a wonderful story, which I think is my all-time favorite.

A long time ago in a far-away land, there was king who had no heir. Now I am sorry to say that this is not a perfectly politically correct story, as in this ancient land, it was a man who would inherit the kingdom, not a woman.

Because he had no male offspring, he sent his squires out to all the villages around, announcing that the next king would be selected not by bloodline, but by an interview. All of the people from round about were invited to come for an interview with the king.

When the appointed day came, they all arrived. Of course they lived in the villages, so they had matted hair, they were dressed in rags, many had long beards, and many had bare feet. Before they could be invited for an interview with the king, they had to go to the royal bathhouse, where they were scrubbed.

Their beards were trimmed or shaved, and they each got a good haircut. When the bathing was over, they were anointed with beautiful oils and scents. Then they were taken to the royal dressing rooms, where they were given new clothes, made out of silk or velvet or satin.

Then the villagers went to the royal banquet chambers, where they could eat anything they desired. A buffet stretched from one end of the hall to the other, with every dish you could imagine from around the world. There were fine wines, too, of every possible variety. The people dined in a style they had never dreamed possible, they drank and they drank, and then out came the musicians and the dancers. There was dancing, and singing, and all kinds of revelry.

Finally, 9 o'clock came, and the guards asked everyone to leave. These poor people from the villages tried to wrap up a leg of mutton, in the beautiful clothes made of silk or satin, but "No," they were told, "you cannot take anything away from here. You can only take what you came with." And so they left the palace in their rags, singing and swaying, with their arms around each other.

The king called in the prime minister. "What happened?" he asked. "I requested you to send out a message to all of my people, so that the next king could be selected by an interview. I've been waiting here the whole day, but nobody came."

The prime minister hung his head in embarrassment. "I'm sorry, my Lord," he said, "but they got so distracted with all of the things you provided—the dancing girls, the music, the food, the drink—that no one remembered to come for the interview."

The king looked at the prime minister in astonishment. "I can't believe this," he said. "If only one of them, one single person, had remembered why he had come, he would have inherited the kingdom. Then all of this would have been his, every day for the rest of his life. But each and every one forgot why he came."

I love this story. When you hear it, does it remind you about anything in your own life? Do you sometimes wonder if you also have forgotten why you came? This is perhaps the most important focus of the coaching relationship: to help people remember why they came.

When a young couple is going to have a child, they have a pure vision of how the child will be raised. They think of the perfect environment in which their son or daughter can grow and prosper, learn, and become their best. But years later, parents become overwhelmed and stressed, from driving kids to soccer practice, and dental appointments, and dealing with missed homework, and they forget why they had the child.

When someone has a vision to start a new business, they raise the capital; they write out their vision statement and their values. But years later, they may find themselves cutting corners to save money, laying off employees, or making deals that are no longer in alignment with their original vision.

People forget why they came.

And of course this is also true in a much bigger way. Here we are, with a few decades to live on the planet. We have gifts to give; maybe we have a message to share. Deep down we have values that are important to us, but so easily we forget why we came.

In Awakening Coaching we have developed an elaborate set of tools to help people relax back deeply enough into who they really are, into their "true nature," that they can remember, perhaps not with thinking but in a more visceral way, who they are and why they came. They remember the gift they came to give.

In a way, this is the point of being coached: to remember who you truly are, to remember why you came, and to remember the gift waiting inside you to be given. This is also the meaning of "awakening."

All that stands in the way is endless distraction.

CHAPTER 24

Freedom from the Cycle of Birth and Death

You seem to be talking a lot about material and personal well-being.
What about those of us who want to break free of the cycle of birth and
death?

David, may I tell you a story?

I lived for several years with my teacher in India. He was not a teacher in the normal sense, as he had no formal teaching to impart and no organization, and he refused to take people on as followers. I would say he was the world's first Awakening Coach. After a while he asked me to go back to America and "share the secret" with my friends. I was not quite sure what he meant.

"What do you want me to do?" I asked.

"Go back to America and tell people about this secret."

"You want me to be a teacher?" I asked in surprise.

"Hmmm, yes, you teach," he mumbled, going back to his newspaper, now bored with the conversation.

I had seen other Westerners become spiritual teachers, and it did not always look so great to me. More potholes than in the Indian roads outside my teacher's house.

"You must be joking!" I retorted.

He looked up from his newspaper. "The truth is a great joke. Now you go and share it with your friends."

I arrived in Seattle, where I had been living before I met him. I got together with a few old friends, then they brought other people, and soon we were having regular meetings with dozens of people.

After a few months like this, I was invited to teach on Orcas Island, which is about two hours by boat from Seattle. It gets very strong winds. A woman had invited me to teach in her house. She told me, "You can have the house to yourself to stay in. We'll have the gathering here, too. I have another house where I will stay." Her house was on a five-acre property, set on a hill facing west, so the winds were coming straight off the Pacific.

During the day, I went into town. All the time I was in India, I had never watched any movies. At that time, there was little access to Western movies in India. Although I used to love films, I had not seen any for about two years. So I went to the video rental store feeling nervous. I didn't want anything violent, anything weird. I was looking for a gentle reintroduction to the world of cinema—like a Disney movie. And then I found one that looked perfect. It had Anthony Hopkins. I like him. It had a very sweet title, *The Silence of the Lambs*. And it had a picture of a butterfly on the cover. Beautiful. I rented it.

After the people had left for the evening, and the woman who owned the house had gone to her other house, I was totally alone on this five-acre lot, in a house that was creaking and swaying in strong winds.

I took my sweet children's movie, with the butterfly on the cover, and put it in the VCR. I sat back to relax.

It turned out to be, to say the least, intense.

The wind was blowing the branch of a tree against the window. *Rat tat tat*. I was starting to get a little freaked. I could not just switch the movie off, because then

I would have had to go to bed not knowing what happened in the story. All I could do was pray for a happy ending.

So here I was, sitting in the living room, all alone, far away from anybody. In front of me was a box. And inside the box was a nightmare.

Now I realized I could go into the story in the box with my attention, and then, "Oh my God! Endless terror." I could also zoom out from the box, and remember "That's Anthony Hopkins. I like him. He is an actor. That's Jodie Foster. They are wearing make-up. It's a movie." I could go in, and I could go out. Zoom in, zoom out. And in this way I survived *The Silence of the Lambs*, entirely alone, on a wind-swept hill, in a creaky house, in the middle of the night.

You become free of the cycle of birth and death in the same way. What is it that is born and dies? It is a body. The body is actually animated earth. Everything about this body has come out of the ground. It is made of carbon and other nutrients that originated in plants. It was created out of another body. It will die. If you are zoomed into "I am David; I am this body," then you are trapped in the cycle of birth and death.

There is also the possibility to zoom out and recognize that limitless consciousness is also present here: without birth, without death, without form. You are also this awareness: aware of David, aware of the fleeting appearance of David.

The way to be free of the cycle of birth and death in this moment, NOW, not in 5 minutes but right now, is to recognize that whatever is happening is being experienced. Sounds are being heard: what hears them? Does that make any sound? Or is it silent? Form, size, color, texture: what is seeing them? Does it have any form? Or is it formless? Limitless? Sensations in the body, contractions of energy, are being felt: what is feeling them? Is that contracted? Or is it open? Is it perhaps love itself?

That is the shortcut to freedom from birth and death: the immediate question, "Who is experiencing all of this?" Then you realize that who you really are has never been trapped in any cycle.

We can say one more thing about this. David is here, isn't he? Every day he gets a little older, moving towards death. And also there is limitless consciousness. It is possible to lean too much into either of these. If you lean too much into David, you are caught in the story, trapped inside *The Silence of the Lambs*, feeling freaked out. If David loses money: Aaahhhh! And if David gets rejected, if David gets sick, if David looks foolish: more Aaaaahhhhhh! Everything becomes serious and tense. But you can also lean too much into emptiness, into spaciousness, and then you are "kind of free," so long as you remain sitting with closed eyes, spine straight, intoning the sound OM.

This has been the error that many Eastern cultures have made: to overemphasize emptiness. Then you lead a life of renunciation. No sex, no money, no relationships, no creativity, no nothing. What is the point of that? Look, we are here, we can enjoy life. The art is to experience the movie, enjoy the acting, and know that it is a movie. Then you are in the game and not in the game at the same time.

This is another good reason to take the concept of "Enlightenment" and flush. We are stepping into a new game now. We are stepping into awakening life. This is not the game that Buddha was playing. It is not the game of renunciation, of celibacy, of living with a begging bowl. This is an exploration of spiritual evolution.

Tell me, David, what are your thoughts about that?

CHAPTER 25

Look, No Ego!

How can I get rid of my ego?

How can you get rid of your what?

The ego. I want to get rid of my ego.

I'm sorry. I didn't catch it. You want to get rid of who? Miko?

No, the ego.

What is it? I've never seen one, so I can't help you get rid of it.
Have you ever seen it? Have you ever heard it? Can you describe it to me?

Not exactly, no. It's not something you see or hear.

Do you know for sure that it exists? If you do not think, or conceptualize, or imagine for a moment, do you know that it exists?

It's when I'm selfish, when I'm fighting for my own interests....

If you go back to the late 19th century, the word "ego" was only used as the first person singular pronoun in Latin. It was Latin for "I." It was used in Freudian circles to describe an aspect of the psyche, and now has entered into common language to try to describe certain self-centered behavior. When the organism gets fascinated by itself and its own processes, instead of experiencing the world around it, we call that function "ego." But it is describing a function, not a thing. You can't find it. And because you cannot find it, there is nothing you can do to get rid of it. There is nothing you can do to make the ego go away, because it does not exist in the first place.

In the same way, if I take this flashlight and move it quickly around and around like this, what do you see?

I see a circle.

And if I stop moving it, where has it gone now? There was no circle, there was just a point of light moving, and we called it a circle. Similarly, there is no ego and there never has been: there is just the movement of thought and feeling. When thoughts and feelings follow certain patterns we say, "That is ego." In any moment of clear seeing, there is nothing called "ego." There is also nothing called "mind." In this moment there is either a thought or no thought, but there is no mind. There is no past here, there is no future here, there is no national debt. These things are all made up, you see? We make them up, we agree to them, and then we try to get rid of them.

That's why we talk here about awakening: not achieving a higher state, or getting rid of lower states, but awakening. It means waking up from things that do not exist. What remains is simple, fresh, and easy.

Now tell me, what do you think about that?

SECTION 5:

Seeya Later

CHAPTER 26

Thanks for Stopping By

All good things must come to an end. I have certainly enjoyed throwing this party for you, from the first idea, to inviting all the guests, to planning the details, to showing you around my world here. I truly hope that you have had a wonderful time, and that you have enjoyed hearing from my friends as much as I do.

I have a little party-favor bag for you, as you make your way out into the evening. First of all, please make sure that you enjoy the readers' website I have created for you. You will find many more video, audio, additional reading, as well as the opportunity to dialog with other guests there. I assume you have been to visit by now, but incase you have not, here is the address again. [36]

Also in the party favor bag is an invitation to go deeper. You might like to receive Awakening Coaching from a certified coach, and you can search for a coach by location or their area of speciality here.[37] You could also join me for a weekend seminar in a city near you. You can find the schedule here.[38] We also have group coaching series that you can access on line from your own home. And then of course you might consider training as an Awakening Coach with us, and you can get all the information here.[39] I wanted to tell you about these things on your way out because you can get a discount on any of these next steps

---

[36] http://better-than-sex.kajabi.com/login

[37] http://awakeningcoachingtraining.com/find-coach

[38] http://awakeningcoachingtraining.com/schedule

[39] http://awakeningcoachingtraining.com/

of the same value as you paid for this book. This essentially makes the book free, if you want to explore more deeply with us.

We talked earlier about the important distinction between techniques and principles, and I'd love to finish our time together by returning to that topic now. I have done my best to give you a good feeling of the practical tools we use in Awakening Coaching. Many of them you can use on your own right away. Some of them you can get more familiar with by practicing them with a coach. But they are all just like kleenex: you can use them to your advantage, but then it is important to also know how to throw them away.

The important thing about kleenex is that it can help you to breathe more easily. Use a kleenex once, and then the smells become more vivid, you can take nice big lung-fulls of air, and feel more alive. Those are important and worthy outcomes. The soiled paper handkerchief you are now left with needs to be disposed of quickly and discreetly. Don't bring it out at dinner parties with great pride, or show it off on a first date. Trust me on this one.

In just the same way, the tools we have explored here, in fact the entire approach of Awakening Coaching, are just like kleenex. They can be useful, but they are not the point. If they do their job well, they will leave you with a restored sense of your true nature as limitless. They will allow you to participate fully in the game of life, no longer with a desperate survival fear driving your every nervous move, but with a sense of ease, a sense of play. They will allow you to show up as love itself, as the life and soul of each and every party.

That is the point, that is worth blogging and tweeting about, that is worth making all kinds of noise about. Don't worry about how you got to breathe easily again, don't worry about the kleenex. Let your enthusiasm be for the intoxicating perfume of the evening jasmine that you are now aware of.

If these tools have proven helpful, or if you now feel inspired to implement them more deeply, then this time has been well spent.

You can bust free of every imagined prison cell that has limited you, and shine in all your glory, just with a small shift of awareness.

You can easily guide others to do the same.

That is the best way I know to use this human adventure.

That is Better than Sex.

ACKNOWLEDGEMENTS

So many people helped out with this book, and the decades of exploration it comes from, that is seems like an impossible task to name them all.

Let's give it a shot.

The original manuscript was delivered as a conversation, between myself and various kind friends. We talked it through together, recorded it, and then it got transcribed. Huge thanks to my dear friends Jonathan Robinson and Matthew Blom for dialoging with me for many hours, as well as to my beloved wife Chameli. Those conversations were transcribed by Kristen Rieger and Myles Aion.

Huge thanks to Myles Aion and David Lasocki for copy editing the final manuscript, and to David Lasocki, Michael Burnstein and Shannon Generazzo for proofreading.

Thanks to our intrepid virtual assistant Shannon Generazzo for preparing the book for final publication, and being generally awesome.

The cover design was created by Tyler Nielson of humanbeam Design. The interior design of the hardcover version is by Marites Bautista.

This book is based on thousands of hours of development of the work of Awakening Coaching over more than twenty years. I am sure I could not even remember all of the brilliant people who have contributed to this evolution, but here are some notable highlights: Oliver Arnold, Verena Hirschmann, Ursula Kauer, Katharina Reider, Sorel Dietzler, Jan Kirby, Suzi April, Connie Kishbaugh, Nikki and Glenn Blackburn, Garrett Stanley, Peter Devries, Olivia Pinto, Tanya Corrin, Marion Meloni and Karen Fritz.

While I love to teach, to coach and to write, I have never been very adept at navigating the giddy world of business. I am hugely grateful to Sorel Dietzler for her generous and loyal contributions to making things run smoothly.

The person who has really made the greatest contribution of all is my friend and manager Michael Burnstein. Thank you Michael for making the noise go away. You are a through and through good man.

Big thanks to everyone who shared their stories. Their names are already to be found in the text of the book.

I am grateful to my agent, Bill Gladstone at Waterside productions, for holding out a big vision in the turbulent world of publishing.

And above all I am always star struck by my beautiful family: Abhi, Shuba, Hanna, Amanda, and my beloved wife Chameli. I am a lucky man.

www.awakeningcoachingtraining.com

Made in the USA
Lexington, KY
09 November 2014